SPRINGBURN TO INVERURIE

A Journey on the Steam and Paraffin Oil Railway

by

Jimmy Brown

Acknowledgements:

My thanks are due to:
Keith Jones for providing the inspiration for this book. To Margaret and
Marianne for their patience. To Alison Cutforth and her staff at the
Springburn Museum for their help and support and to Bob Gray and Andy
Hume for filling in the gaps.

ISBN   0 9522706 0 9

Published by: Jimmy Brown
                     6 Strathburn Gardens
                     Inverurie
                     AB51 4RY

All photographs from the Jimmy Brown collection except where noted.

Cover photo:
Caledonian Railway 123 passing St Rollox station, Glasgow, in about 1958
with two preserved Caledonian Railway coaches.   *(Springburn Museum)*

Buchanan Street Boy

DELIVERING the papers one chill March Monday morning in Second Avenue, in the Millerston district of Glasgow, I knew something was up the minute I saw my brother, Bill, racing towards me on my brand-new BSA bike. Bill would never take the liberty of a shot on my new bike unless the matter was urgent.

The year was 1938 and I had just left school and taken a job delivering papers and telegrams from Millerston post office until I was summoned to join the London Midland & Scottish Railway. I would be the third generation to work on the railway and no other occupation had ever been considered in my family.

Brother Bill's message was urgent indeed. A letter had arrived by first post that morning requiring my presence at LMS Headquarters, 302 Buchanan Street, at 9am. The time was now 7.30am so there wasn't a second to lose. It would never do for a budding railwayman to be late for work on his first day. I threw the bag of papers and notebook of customers' names at Bill and jumped on my bike to rush home and change in time to meet the deadline.

I made it, and was directed by a rather supercilious clerk, who seemed singularly unimpressed by my barely-five-foot height and short trousers, to Buchanan Street Passenger Station, where I was to start work as a Telegraph Messenger.

My first week's duty was from 10am to 8pm with a two-hour break from 2 to 4. Saturday had an early finish when I operated from 10am to 6pm with only a twenty minute break to snatch something to eat. Second week I was on night shift, which meant seven turns from 10pm to 6am, starting on Sunday night and finishing the following Sunday morning, when you had 24 hours off before starting your next week's early turn at 6am on Monday morning. How you got home at 6am on a Sunday morning was strictly your concern. There was no public transport and if you hadn't a bike you walked.

One lad who lived in Giffnock thought he would snatch a few hours' sleep in an empty train till the trams started running but while he slept the train was shunted out to the carriage sidings at Stepps and he was aghast to awake far out in the country. He had no idea where he was but found the main road and got his bearings from a Sunday morning stroller. He had only his tram fare from the town to Giffnock so he walked from Stepps to the city centre before boarding his tram home. Meantime his worried parents were telephoning the office at Buchanan

Street demanding to know where he was.

Night shift was my favourite. I had never been up all night before and clearly remember my excitement as the big office clock's hands moved towards midnight, but I hadn't much time for clock-watching.

I had to make two trips to Glasgow Central with telegrams each night, and several heart-in-mouth runs through the huge, darkened Buchanan Street Goods Yard, where rats scuttled in the gloom, with messages for the Delivery Office at K Shed, near Dobbie's Loan. I also had to make occasional forays among the tenements of Cowcaddens and Garscube Road to call out linemen to attend to signal failures. The streets were quiet at that time of night with only midden (rubbish) squads about, with their huge Clydesdale horses and guttering helmet lamps, and street-cleaning gangs hosing away the day's dirt. Coffee stalls at St Vincent Place and at the junction of Cowcaddens and Port Dundas Road served the few late-night stragglers.

I discovered how to operate the traffic lights in Renfield Street by jumping on the rubber pad in the roadway and took a boyish delight in switching the lights in the face of on-coming traffic. But I soon abandoned that pastime after I turned the lights to red in front of a big Post Office van one wet night and sent him into a wild skid.

After my twenty-minute break at 2am I was sent down to the dark passenger station to help the night watchman, old Sandy Birnie, load newspapers and mail into the first train of the day, the 4.45am to Braidwood. Sandy had served in the army out in India in Queen Victoria's reign and he enlivened the waits between vans with tales of his adventures. I particularly liked to hear about his pet monkey, Mick, and still remember my sadness when I learned it had disappeared from a troop train taking Sandy from one part of India to another.

In return for my help Sandy gave me a few of the free papers he got from the vanmen to take up to the office. These were grabbed by the clerks and it was seldom I had anything more interesting to take home than one of the duller 'quality' papers of the day. The papers, mail and vans of lovely fresh-smelling bread for the Highlands and Islands left around 11pm and I well remember my mother's incredulity when I took a free paper home one night with the next day's date. As I recognise now, she pretended not to believe it and appeared very impressed with her wee son's cleverness.

After the Braidwood left with its sleepy workmen passengers at 4.45, Sandy and I took a barrow-load of papers round to the next train, the 5.55am for Perth, or the 'Parly' as it was called. Government regulations compelled all railways to run one train each day in both directions which stopped at every station. These slow trains became known as 'Parlys', and the 5.55am was ours. But my night's work was still far from finished, even then. I had the office fires to bank and clean and had to light the fires in the mess room and the public counter office down in the station. Then I had to set the train arrival boards before I finally crawled home to bed.

The 1938 Bellahouston Park Empire Exhibition fell in my first year at work and I was sitting with old Sandy in the paper train one morning when I heard a big steam engine clanking into the station with a train.

"What's that?" I asked Sandy.

"Don't know," he replied.

"Probably empty carriages..."

I looked around the end of the platform to where the new arrival was standing in a blaze of light with passengers hanging out of every window peering into the dark station.

"It's no' empty carriages at aw," I cried to Sandy.

"It's a train fu' o' folk!"

"Well, they kin just bide where they are," said Sandy complacently, puffing at his pipe.

"This station disny open till half past four."

I went round to the packed train and as soon as the passengers saw my uniform I became the centre of attraction. The train was an Exhibition excursion from the Midlands of England that had somehow been re-directed round to us.

"Where are we...?"

"Can we get out here...?"

"Where can we get a cup of tea...?"

These were some of the questions clamoured at me.

Old Sandy remained entrenched in the paper train out of sight so I answered as best I could.

They were in Glasgow, but the station did not open till 4.30, and they might as well stay where they were because there was nowhere to go anyway. Lastly, there was no tea to be had. The coffee stall closed at 2.30 and the station buffet did not open till 7am.

One worried passenger took me aside.

"Could you not rustle up just one cup of tea...? he pleaded.

"My wife suffers from travel-sickness and she's feeling pretty low..."

I had the best part of a quarter of tea and a tin of condensed milk in my locker upstairs but I risked being mobbed if I appeared on that platform with tea.

"Listen," I said.

"Take your wife round to the first class waiting room on Platform One and I will see what I can do... but don't tell anybody else!"

I quietly made a pot of tea and took it round to Platform One but when I entered the first class waiting room it was a seething mass of thirsty passengers. The word had got out somehow! There was nothing for it but to make tea to the limit of my meagre resources. I made no charge but when I counted my tips afterwards I was astonished to find I had made fifteen shillings (75p), practically a week's wages for me at that time. I have often thought since that only lack of supplies prevented me from making my fortune that night.

While the night shift remained my favourite, the day shifts offered more opportunities to 'swadge', as the practice of carrying passengers' bags for tips was called. Swadging was sternly discouraged and notices were periodically posted threatening the direst consequences if we did not desist forthwith, but we swadged away regardless. I got the fright of my young life one day when I opened a door on an incoming Inverness train to gaze into the stern features of my boss, George Fraser. I took off like an Olympic runner round the back of the Parcels Office and spent a day or two in fear and trepidation lest I be summoned to his presence for a good dressing down at least or maybe even — horrors! — the sack!

But I never heard any more about it. No doubt Mr Fraser though I'd been punished enough with the fright I'd got.

There were four porters on each shift to carry bags but at busy times there would obviously be more bags to be carried than there were porters and this was when we boys came into our own at the swadging. The real porters would glower at us and make threats but they would not actually stoop so low as to take a bag from a boy — all except Big Davie Stevenson, that is. He would stop at nothing to get a tip.

One morning I was passing the front of the station very early when a taxi drew up. There was still an hour to the first main-line train of the day — the 7.20am to Aberdeen — and the porters were still in their bothy, so I opened the taxi door.

The passenger was a lady with a large hamper. It was a bit of a struggle for me but I got the hamper out of the taxi and on to a barrow. The lady gave me a shilling (5p) and told me to put her hamper in the guard's van of the Aberdeen train. I was bending to lift the barrow's shafts when Big Davie Stevenson appeared.

"I'll take that," he said, pushing me roughly aside.

"OK," I muttered rebelliously. "It's for the Aberdeen van."

"That's the passenger over at the booking office."

It was maybe just as well for me Big Davie appeared when he did for he had quite a struggle pushing the barrow with the hamper up the steep slope to the Aberdeen train at Platform Two. I watched developments with great interest and not a little apprehension from behind the information board. What would happen if Big Davie discovered I had the tip for the job? The passenger's shilling burned a hole in my pocket. But all went well for me. Big Davie loaded the hamper into the van and hovered round the window of the lady's compartment for a while before giving her up in disgust as that hazard of a railway porter's life — a non-tipping passenger.

The stationmaster, Tom Crichton, made occasional forays from his office dressed in his top hat and tails, with a flower in his button-hole, and when VIPs were travelling he would greet them personally at the front of the station and escort them to their seats. Other not-so-VIPs were prisoners en route to Peterhead and we used to watch from a safe distance as they sat hand-cuffed to warders on each side in their reserved compartment.

Finding passengers' reserved seats was another lucrative sideline, as was whistling up cabs from the rank outside in Port Dundas Road. Messrs Paterson had the concession to ply for hire within the station but the independent taximen could not enter the station unless summoned by a railway employee. When a train arrived, Patersons' cabs were soon taken up and passengers would queue under the 'Taxi' sign at Platform Five. By a quirk of the station architecture, the waiting passengers could not see the line of independent cabs outside, and it was a simple matter for we boys to offer: "Taxi, sir...?" A few steps round the corner of the building took us into view of the cabs and in seconds we had a taxi up the ramp to the rather astonished passengers, who usually signified their gratitude in the customary manner.

Tips? Well, the usual thing was a sixpence ($2^1/_2$p) which might not seem much in these inflation-ridden days but in 1938 it could buy me five Player's cigarettes and a fish supper for my tea. Only a snack supper, of course, for the best quality cost fourpence, but I was a regular patron at the old-fashioned sawdust-floored chipper at the top of Renfield Street. I remember once asking the rather weary proprietor whether he was frying new potatoes yet. The old man seemed to consider my question superfluous, for he replied with heavy irony:

"You DID say a thrupenny snack...?"

But his sarcasm flew high over my young head.

"Aye, that's right," I said in puzzlement, thinking the old duffer must be going off his head.

"Ah was jist wonderin' if thae wur new tatties..."

But he ignored me and I never did find out.

The station staff at Buchanan Street in 1938 seems enormous from this distance. Apart from Stationmaster Tom Crichton and his office staff, each shift had an Inspector and a Foreman Porter in addition to four platform porters, parcel porters, carriage cleaners, shunters, and so on. There was also a railway policeman on each shift to keep the station clear of urchins and other undesirables.

Excursion trains ran on summer Sundays to beauty spots like Crieff and St Fillans and here station staff was kept to a minimum. There was no luggage to carry so there was no opportunity for swadging but one bright spark worked out a very profitable racket. These excursion trains had no class so it was a simple matter to lock up the first class compartments early on and release them near starting time to courting couples, who were usually suitably grateful.

In those far-off days I frequently made more in tips from swadging than my weekly wage of sixteen shillings (80p). My adolescent tastes were simple — the best seats in the cinema, Cadbury's Dairy Milk chocolate to eat and Churchman's Number One cigarettes to smoke. I thought I had it made. But as we entered 1939 my life of luxury collapsed when I was taken into the office to become a Check Boy, the first step on what turned out to be a long ladder of promotion.

One Foot On The Ladder!

Although Buchanan Street was by far the smallest main-line station in Glasgow, with only five platforms, it had the largest telegraph office to cope with the flow of telegrams to and from the head office at 302 Buchanan Street. The telephone was not in general use then and the bulk of railway messages passed over the company's network of single-needle telegraph instruments. Older readers may remember the curious tinkling noise that could be heard coming from booking offices on wayside stations. This was the telegraph instrument and all stations and signal boxes were connected. Messages were transmitted in the Morse Code and I was completely baffled the first time I entered Buchanan Street Telegraph Office to see some thirty male and female clerks seated on stools round a large room rattling away at these noisy things. However, once I learned the code I realised that a clerk's hand could be detected on the instrument as surely as his voice or handwriting.

Coming home from South Africa after the Second World War, I took advantage of a train stop at Carlisle to visit the telegraph office and call up my brother, Frank, who was then working at Buchanan Street, on the instrument. The line ran through Glasgow Central Telegraph Office and a clerk there turned to a colleague to say: "That's Jimmy Brown" as soon as my hand touched the key.

As a Check Boy I was still a uniformed Telegraph Messenger but instead of delivering telegrams outside I was kept inside to collect the wires as they came off the instruments and telephones and sort them onwards. There were two of us and we alternated 8am to 5.30pm one week and 9am to 6.30pm the next, with a 6am to 2pm shift every second Sunday. In between times we practiced the Morse Code on two dummy instruments and in time we were even allowed to send a real telegram to some wayside station on the Largs line. Next step was to receive a message on the 'T', or one-word-at-a-time principle under the supercilious supervision of one of the Junior Clerks, whose seniority in the art could not have been much more than my own. After passing an examination at the age of sixteen I was taken on to the Salaried Staff as a Junior Telegraph Clerk, although I thought it was a bit of an Irish promotion at the time since my pay went down from £1 a week as a Check Boy to 17/- (85p) a week as a Junior Telegraph Clerk.

But no matter. I was on the second rung of the ladder and in no time at all I could read at the top speed as well as anyone else in the office.

The Second World War had started by this time and our work load in the Telegraph Office increased enormously. The line to Carlisle was manned twenty four hours a day — half an hour sending and half an hour receiving. My time was spent mainly on the less busy lines like the Oban and Ayr wires but I remember yet the glow of pride I felt one night when the supervisor, old Davie Blair, asked me to take the Carlisle wire while the regular man had his break. Now I knew how General Montgomery felt when he was promoted to Field Marshall!

Under the supervision of one of the older lads, Bob Gray — who will appear later in this narrative as the legendary Black Bob — I learned how to chaff the operators at the other end — especially the girls at places like Kilmarnock and Ayr. A form of shorthand was used here in that we sent the letter 'I' for the affirmative in place of 'aye' or 'yes', letter 'U' for you, and so on, while you sent 'MIM' to show appreciation if the

11

party at the other end said something funny. I also learned how to swear in the Morse Code. Don't ask me why, but the most offensive thing you could say to the operator at the other end was 'PQ'. It has a fine old swing to it when you rattle it out but the origin of the practice remains a mystery.

With the strain of the war I was promoted into the Grade Five link at Buchanan Street while still only seventeen. The hours were long, with 48 hours per week the minimum. Night shift involved seven turns adding up to 60 hours and I remember one week when I worked from 9am to 11pm Monday to Saturday. It seems incredible now but some of us actually developed corns on our fingers from the many hours of continuous writing.

One Spring day in 1941 I was sending a long message to Connel Ferry, on the Oban line. The wire was located in Connel Ferry West Junction signal box and the signalman could only read 'T', or at the slow, learner's speed. After we passed the message safely I enquired what the weather was like at his end. He said it was a glorious day, with the birds singing outside, and I expressed the hope that the weather would hold because I proposed to take a trip up that way next day.

My Aunt Kate was blind and she had been evacuated to Onich, near Ballachulish, at the start of the war along with many of Glasgow's blind folk. When I had a day off I used to go up to see her, although it was a long journey and I only had time enough for a hurried meal with my aunt at Ballachulish Ferry before setting off back to Glasgow.

I told the signalman at Connel Ferry all this over the wire and he suggested I pop in to see him next day as I would have an hour to wait at Connel Ferry before catching the train up the Ballachulish branch.

The next day I duly presented myself at the signalbox where I was made very welcome by my new-found friend, John Ferguson by name. The floor was scrubbed white, the levers sparkled and the woodwork shone in Connel Ferry West, I can tell you. And I was touched when John led me over to a corner where he had a spotless table cloth spread with a sandwich snack and a flask of tea and all the trimmings. I would be having lunch with my aunt but it would have been churlish to have refused John's hospitality and, in any case, I was only seventeen at the time with the appetite of youth.

There wasn't much time to spend at Connel Ferry on the way back but John Ferguson was there with his collie dog to see me safely on to the Glasgow train. He also had half-a-dozen eggs for me to take home — a rare treat in wartime when you were lucky to see an egg a month in the big cities.

Thus was the pattern set. Every time I made the trip to Ballachulish Ferry I used the telegraph to warn my friends at Connel Ferry — I say friends because by this time I had got to know John's mate, Ewen McKinnon, and no matter who was on duty, my snack was always laid out for me in their signal box when I got off the Glasgow train. There was little I could do in return for this lavish hospitality, but pipe tobacco was a little easier to get in Glasgow than it was in Connel and I usually managed to have something with me to offer in return.

The ex-Highland Railway 'Clans' and 'Castles' were the main stay of the Oban line when I started going along the branch. The Oban portion was worked from Glasgow Buchanan Street to Stirling as part of the 7.20am to Aberdeen. From Stirling the HR engines took over and I have fond memories of 'Urquhart Castle' struggling up the bank from Balquhidder piloted by — of all things! — a Drummond 0-6-0 Caley 'Jumbo'. I remember listening to the exhaust of the two engines out of the carriage window and to my youthful imagination it sounded as if the big 'woof' of the Highland engine was telling the stuttering Caley 'Jumbo' to get out of the way. Motive power was short in those days, although before I finished taking my jaunts up the Oban line the ubiquitous LMS 'Black Fives' had taken over. This happened in November, 1942, when I was called up for service in the Royal Naval Patrol Service — as a telegraphist, of course!

The call-up drained the telegraph office staff as men of military age joined up. A few went into the Army and the Royal Air Force but the Royal Navy seemed to cotton on to the fact that we railway telegraph clerks were already trained in Morse and it was a simple matter to convert us from Single Needle to Buzzer. At any rate, five of us were called up for service in the Navy regardless of any contrary preference. When I registered for call-up I stated a preference for RAF Ground Staff — something reasonably safe with a nice uniform — but in the event I received an Army medical and got called up to the Navy.

My wartime adventures have no place here but I did enjoy the long journey down the LNER East Coast Main Line to the Royal Naval Patrol Service Central Depot at Lowestoft. Overnight to Peterborough, and from there it was sheer magic along the rural lines of the Midland and Great Northern Joint Railway through places with strange-sounding names like King's Lynn, Melton Constable and Great Yarmouth. An ancient 4-4-0 up front hauled a string of truly venerable coaches. The seats were thinly upholstered — something like our present-day Class

158 Sprinters — there was only one radiator placed length-wise between two compartments, the coaches were gas-lit and the doors into the corridor swung outwards on hinges.

We stopped every few miles while the railway staff and local population caught up with the news of the day. There was no hurry at all, at all, and it was all of six hours before we finally meandered into Lowestoft Central Station.

On leave prior to going overseas I made one last trip up the Oban line. I had no way of warning my friends at Connel and when I walked into Connel Ferry West, John Ferguson was mortified because he had no food ready for me. I assured him it didn't matter but he insisted on leaving me in charge of his precious signal box while he hurried down to his lineside cottage to get something for me to eat. I must have looked a strange sight standing there in my sailor's suit praying that nothing would happen before John got back. As it happened, Buchanan Street came on the wire with a message of more than 100 words, which I was able to take off at my telegraph clerk's speed, much to John's relief when he returned, for it would have taken him most of his shift to get it at his 'T' speed.

Back home after the war we were all interviewed by the-then Operating Manager of the LMS, Mr J. N. Phillipps. I knew that name well, after writing it hundreds of times on telegrams. It used to occur to me as I wearily pencilled it for the umpteenth time that day that Mr Phillipps would save us all a lot of unnecessary work — and pencils! — if he would shorten the spelling to Philips!

But we ex-servicemen were heroes at the time and Mr Phillipps made a point of welcoming us back to the LMS personally and asking us which direction we thought our careers should take.

I had enjoyed my time in the Telegraph Office but the job really had little prospects. There were ten clerks on Grade Five, six on Grade Four, two on Grade Three and only one — the clerk-in-charge — on Grade One.

So opportunities for promotion were limited and when I had Mr Phillipps in my sights I asked him for a transfer to the Control side of things. He nodded his assent to one of his assistants and that was that.

I went to war as a Telegraph Clerk and returned to the LMS Railway as an Assistant Controller.

Control Capers

A sunny day in May, 1946, and I reported to St Rollox Control to take up my new career.

Based in a former cattle shed behind St Rollox Works, the St Rollox Control area stretched from Coatbridge Junction to Dunblane North on the main line and down into the former Caledonian terminus at Buchanan Street. It also covered the Lanarkshire and Dunbartonshire section from Balloch to Bridgeton Cross through 'The Hole', as the section through Glasgow Central Low Level was called.

The Shift Controller at Class One had overall responsibility but he concerned himself mainly with Buchanan Street Goods Station, St Rollox Top Yard and Robroyston East Yard and the surrounding branches, like the original Caledonian line through St Rollox West End to the banks of the Forth and Clyde Canal at Port Dundas. He also had an exchange yard at Sighthill for handing and receiving traffic from that other railway, the LNER (Late and Never Early, as we sniggered among ourselves).

The North Board had a Class Three Controller and a Class Four Assistant Controller to run the section from Coatbridge to Dunblane, and the L & D had the same, while the six-man shift was completed by a Class Five Assistant Controller to keep the records and assist generally. In addition, there were two Plant Controllers on day shift to regulate the supply of empty vehicles.

There were three shifts to man the office twenty four hours a day, seven days a week, and I thought my luck had run out when I was allocated to Andrew Jack's shift.

Andrew Jack was a first class railwayman. Let there be no doubt about that. But it remains a fact that he was not an easy man to work with. He always seemed to be in a bad mood — possibly he had an ulcer, like so many after years of working long hours on awkward shifts. Who knows? But he had no sense of humour and perhaps that was what made me play a trick on him when, in the fullness of time, I moved on from St Rollox Control. I got a stick and a piece of string and made up a primitive whip which I sent to him anonymously through the railway mail labelled 'For Use As Required'. The rest of the shift had been tipped off and there was an assured audience when Andrew Jack opened up his parcel. Turning red in the face, he threw the whip into the fire with a mighty oath, uttering assorted threats against the sender.

The story went round the bothies like lightning and ever after that Andrew Jack was known as 'The Whup'. The men out on the line displayed remarkable ingenuity in dragging whips and whipping into their everyday working conversations. Dialogues like this:

Andrew Jack to Yard Foreman: "Can you take in a train i' bogies...?"

Yard Foreman to Andrew Jack: "Och aye, Andra. Jist 'whip' them in!"

Many years later I took a notion to visit the main — indeed, by that time, the only — Control Room at ScotRail House in Glasgow. There was only one man on duty who remembered me from my St Rollox Control days but he gave me the VIP treatment, conducting me round like Royalty and introducing me proudly to each man as:

"This is Jimmy Brown — you know, The Man That Sent The Whip To Andrew Jack".

But apart from Andrew Jack I have many happy memories of my time at St Rollox Control.

The Shift Controller had a primitive type of switchboard with which he could plug into any of the many telephone lines that reached our office from every part of our territory, but we had to use the phones on the walls right round the room, and for a time I was assistant to Sandy Clark on the North Board.

'A legend in his own lifetime', Sandy Clark had a pawky sense of humour that did much to off-set the grumpiness of Andrew Jack, and when that worthy went over the score he was well able to put him in his place.

Our patch was centred mainly on Greenhill where we had an Up and Down Yard. We also had a fair sized yard at Stirling and a major port installation and motive power depot at Grangemouth. Traffic from the north gravitated to Greenhill and from there we worked it forward to Mossend, in the Motherwell Control area, and Polmadie, south of the Clyde.

A network of daily freight services catered for the traffic arising at the various points in the system. This was worked to the nearest marshalling yard as a matter of routine without any direction from us.

In addition, sets of men with engines came off the sheds at regular intervals throughout the twenty four hours. These were called 'conditionals' in that they were allocated work according to the conditions prevailing at the time. Each marshalling yard phoned details of the traffic on hand every two hours to Control and we arranged trips to adjacent areas as necessary. In those halcyon days we often had more traffic than we could handle and sometimes it became necessary to put a stop on traffic going into a yard to give the staff of shunters a chance to clear their feet.

One night Sandy and I came on duty to find that Polmadie had stopped the traffic some hours previously. This had reacted on our yard at Greenhill to the extent that the yard foreman was complaining he couldn't turn a wheel. A very serious situation indeed and one that called for drastic measures.

Sandy considered the position carefully before ringing up his opposite number at Polmadie Control, Jock Barrowman. To my surprise, he made no mention of the mess at Greenhill, talking merely about the weather and other matters of no consequence.

"It's a strange thing, Jock," said Sandy.

"But you and I have worked thegither for many years and yet we've never met... whit aboot fixin' a gemme o' bools for the next early shift...?"

"Great idea, Sandy," replied Jock enthusiastically.

"Why don't we do just that...?"

Details were fixed, and then Sandy moved in for the kill.

"Now Jock" he wheedled.

"Whit aboot takin' in wan train frae Greenhill... jist WAN train...?"

"Well, awright then," agreed Barrowman reluctantly.

"Bit jist WAN train, mind!"

Sandy sprang into action. He took the biggest engine we had available — a W.D. 2-10-0 — hung around sixty wagons on it, put a banker in the rear to shove it up the hill to Cumbernauld, and let it rip down through Coatbridge to Polmadie, where it landed with something of the impact of a German V2 Rocket.

I watched all this, horrified. When Barrowman said 'WAN train' he meant the usual load for a Caley 'Jumbo' — equal to thirty of goods. What he got was over two such trains, yet, strictly speaking, Sandy had only sent him 'WAN train' as agreed.

Minutes later the Polmadie phone nearly jumped off the wall and I listened on the extension as Barrowman gave Sandy Clark a succinct and comprehensive resume of his character, making frequent references to his parents having apparently neglected to get married before he was born.

Sandy enjoyed this hugely, and when Barrowman finally ran out of steam, he said:

"Now, Jock, what aboot this gemme o' bools next week...?"

"Ach, tae hell wi' you and yer bools," roared Jock, hanging up his phone with a bang.

Next night they were as friendly as ever, although the proposed game of bowls never did take place, nor did Sandy and Jock ever meet face to face.

Sandy Clark was a menace when girl friends of the younger set came on the phone. If he answered he would say something like:

"Jimmy...? Aye, haud oan. He's jist scrubbin' the flerr the noo... he'll be wi' ye as soon as he's dried his hauns..."

Either that or he would roar out in a loud voice clearly audible at the other end of the line:

"Jimmy! Here's the wife oan frae the Cadora...?"

Wife...?

Cadora...?

Many a promising romance foundered as a result of Sandy's misplaced wit but in spite of his attempts at sabotage, some of the younger lads just back from the forces got married and when, in due course, their wives had babies, Sandy would congratulate them with a leer.

"Whit did ye get...?" he would enquire solicitously,

"A plain frontit yin or an ornamental frontit yin...?"

One of our guards, Basil Merson, had formed a liaison with a canteen lady at Carlisle, and had taken to going down to see her on his days off, telling his wife he was on duty. But Mrs Merson got suspicious and started calling us up late at night to check what shift her husband was on.

This was a bit of a nuisance, since it meant ploughing through reams of guards' rosters, but nobody said anything till one night she came on when we were in the middle of a derailment.

Sandy answered the phone and when the good lady announced herself as "Basil Merson's wife..." Sandy replied: "Which wan...?"

The poor woman hung up without another word and we never heard from her again.

Another guard, Jock Bell, had an extremely gullible wife and when he had exhausted his pocket money for the week he would tap her for five bob (25p) to buy a new shunting pole, and when really desperate he would beg sixpence ((2^1/2p) to buy paraffin for his lamp.

The guards were a mixed bunch and I remember an encounter I had with one of them — Geordie Cushnie by name — very well.

The 4.45am paper train from Buchanan Street to Braidwood had been taken off at the start of the Second World War and never reinstated. Instead, two or three covered goods vans and a brake van left the Cattle Bank, outside our office, for Lockerbie, in its place, and it was the custom for the junior man on the night shift to go out and give the guard a hand in return for a few of the free papers he got from the van drivers.

One night I went out to do this duty for old Geordie Cushnie, a rather taciturn lad nearing retirement age. To my horror, Geordie was unhappy with the papers he got from the vanmen and took a hand-full from some of the bigger bundles to make up the numbers. He knew each signalman's preference and laid them out along one side of his brake van — a Glasgow Herald for Sighthill Junction, Daily Record for Germiston, Express for Robroyston West, and so on. Geordie threw out the paper of his choice to each signalman as he passed along the line. Not very honest, of course, but otherwise an excellent service.

The only light in the brake van was provided by Geordie's hand lamp and it should not be surprising that I picked up the wrong bundle of papers one night and disrupted Geordie's distribution routine as far as Lockerbie. I got my character from Geordie next night, and no mistake, and there the story ended until one night about three months later when I found myself on the same duty with Geordie once again.

I wondered what my reception might be as I took a seat in the dark brake van to await the arrival of the first newspaper van. Geordie blethered away quite happily, much to my relief, until we got on to the subject of Control Office staff.

"Ye get some right eejits in there," he said scornfully.

"Don't ye...?"

I hastened to agree, wondering what was coming next.

"They sent wan oot tae me aboot three months ago," he went on, as I listened with mounting horror.

"A mair stupit-lukkin' neep ah've never seen..." and he went on to give me what I can only describe as a completely unbiased report on my abilities, character and future prospects. Obviously Geordie did not connect me with the subject under discussion and I listened with fascination and not a little glee until he finally unwound.

"Ah, but you're lucky, Geordie," I ventured when he eventually fell silent.

"You only see that sort of lad once in a while — I have to work with them all the time!"

Control work was a fascinating experience. No matter what mess you left behind you at the end of a shift, the picture when you next booked on would be totally different.

Passenger trains ran to the timetable so we didn't tamper with them unless there was something far wrong like an engine failure — something that rarely happened in the days of steam.

Our work was with the goods traffic and at the end of each shift Sandy would compile a list of the engines at work for handing over to the next North Board Controller, Andrew Boult, or 'Sir Adrian' as Sandy called him.

Sandy Clark endeared himself to me by handing me the list each day and asking:

"Does that meet with your approval...?"

Considering my juniority it didn't really matter what I thought, but it was nice of Sandy to ask and I remember him kindly for it.

Frank On The Footplate

My two brothers, Bill and Frank, had followed me into the LMS. Bill entered the commercial side before going into the Public Relations department, while Frank moved on to the motive power after a couple of years in Buchanan Street Telegraph Office.

Bill's work was very different from mine but Frank used to come home, tired and weary, after a long stint on the footplate to tell me what he thought about those idiots in the Control!

His first firing turn was on an old Caley 'Bogie' (Pickersgill 4-4-0) piloting a holiday special from Buchanan Street to Aberdeen one Glasgow Fair Friday. In those days it was quite common to run as many as twenty specials to Aberdeen on Fair Friday and motive power was at a premium. I watched Frank slogging away as the train struggled up the gradient from Buchanan Street past our window. He hadn't time to look up and later he told me he'd shovelled more coal out of the window that day than he got into the fire!

Frank's adventures on the footplate deserve a book to themselves but I remember particularly one night he was firing a train of cattle from Merklands to Kittybrewster. They had five trucks fitted with the vacuum brake next the engine, an LMS 'Black Five' 4-6-0, to give them extra braking power. But coming down the glen at Cumbernauld the vacuum pipe on the fifth vehicle jumped off its stud, causing the air to rush into the pipe and apply the brakes.

Both men left the footplate — a bad mistake — and went back along the train. In the light of their flickering paraffin lamp they soon spotted the errant vacuum bag hanging down and without stopping to think, Frank ducked between the buffers to slam it back onto its stud.

Trouble was, they had left the vacuum ejector working on the engine and as soon as Frank put the bag back onto the stud the brakes came off and the 'Black Five' started away by itself.

20

Both men set off after it at once, with Frank well in the lead, but he tripped over a signal wire and measured his near-six-foot length in the ballast. The driver — a wee fat man — overtook him while he was getting up but Frank soon regained the lead and fortunately managed to reach the footplate of their 'Black Five' before any damage was done.

"Would have made quite a splatter at Larbert," said Frank thoughtfully when he told me about it later.

In my day guards were universally hated by footplate men throughout the railway.

First of all, they had a nice comfortable van to ride in at the back of the train, with a lovely coal stove to keep them warm. Second, they were in charge of the train, although it was the footplate men at the front who had all the hard work to do. With the heat in their van they were liable to fall asleep and this could have dire consequences for the locomotive crew — especially in those days when most goods trains were loose-coupled with only the brake van at the rear to help hold the train on a falling gradient.

Frank was working a train to Buchanan Street one night when the guard fell asleep and the train ran away with the engine. Fortunately, there was a spare brake van marshalled as the first vehicle in the train and Frank was able to climb over the tender and swing himself into this van and get the brake on — otherwise they would have ended up out in the Cowcaddens!

Some of the more religious engine-men used to maintain that there would be no trains in Heaven because you could not run a train without a guard. Indeed one such has left us a few lines of poetry to emphasise the point.

Epitaph For A Goods Guard

Sleep well, thou faithful goods guard
Sleep well, thou railwayman
Just lie as peaceful in your grave
As you did in your van

Frank had more than his share of trouble with cattle trains, like the time he was taking a special to Carlisle when one of the trucks burst open as they were passing through Lockerbie and some of the beasts fell out on to the platform.

An enquiry was held at Carlisle and the guard stepped forward to give his evidence.

He was obviously conscious of the suspicion that he might have been asleep so he thought to disabuse the panel of that idea at once.

"Oh aye, ah wis keepin' a guid look-out..." he maintained.

"Ah saw the coos staunin' oan the platform at Lockerbie — an' ah kin mind wonderin' whaur they were gaun'!"

In face of such convincing evidence it should not be surprising that this particular guard lived to run many more trains.

One of Frank's early firing turns took him to Larbert with a conditional goods. They had just replenished their tender at the water column and were awaiting the signal when Frank thought he would brew up. The driver waited till he was finished before he asked him:

"Where did ye get the water for yer tea... the tender?"

Frank laughed scornfully. At seventeen he was still green — but not that green. Tenders accumulated all kinds of rubbish through the years, like oily waste and dead rats — there was even one tender at St Rollox reputed to house a live eel.

"Nae fear," Frank assured the driver confidently.

"Ah took it frae the water column."

"Did ye...?" chuckled the driver.

"That water comes straight frae the Forth & Clyde Canal!"

Later that shift the driver thought he would he would have his snack while they were waiting the right-away at another signal. He had some tasty bacon and egg sandwiches and he handed the throttle over to Frank while he warmed them on the firing shovel in the mouth of the firebox.

Frank was understandably on the alert — it was the first time he'd had such a responsibility in his short career — and he kept his eyes glued to the signal. When the signal dropped he swung the throttle open at once, causing the driver's tasty sandwiches to vanish into the firebox with the first blast of steam going up the chimney.

In those days we often had more traffic than we could handle and it wasn't all that unusual for Grangemouth to turn out a big Caley 'Jumbo' (0-6-0 3F) for the long run to Carlisle. Mostly, though, it was LMS 'Black Fives' and Class 8 2-8-0s, although after the railways bought the wartime Austerity 2-8-0s and 2-10-0s from the government our trusty Class 8s were taken south and we were left with the inferior ex-W.D. engines.

Enginemen and guards working to Carlisle slept in the dormitory there and worked back next day. The climb back up Beattock Summit was something to be dreaded, especially by the firemen. Banking engines were kept at Beattock but it must be said that some of the crews were bone idle and often did little more than keep the buffers together.

It got so bad that signalmen in a box half way up were instructed to keep a look-out and report any engine not really trying.

My brother Frank said he always had his head down shovelling all the way up and the only way he knew they were at the half-way mark was when he felt a surge of power coming from the rear, only to die away again after they passed the box with its vigilant signalmen.

One turn Frank liked was the 3.40pm Glasgow Buchanan Street to Carlisle on a Saturday afternoon. This was a fully-fitted express goods and if they got round to Carstairs in time they got a clear path to Carlisle in front of the 4pm passenger ex Glasgow Central, with the result that they had their engine put by and their feet up by 7pm.

The return leg on the Sunday, however, seldom took less than twelve hours although the lines were relatively quiet. Why? Well, on Saturday the men were guaranteed their eight hours pay no matter how soon they got to Carlisle while on Sundays they were paid their actual time worked and, as Frank's driver used to remind him when he complained at their snail's pace:

"Every tick's a tick and a half!"

Signalmen's Timekeeper

With the Spring of 1947 I wasn't sorry to be taken off Andrew Jack's shift to take over as Signalman's and Porter's Timekeeper. For one thing, it was a nine-to-five job. I loved my work in the Control Room but the shifts were a bit of a bind. You really had only one week in three — the early turn — when you could have any sort of a social life and, at 22, I was a bit young for this monk-like existence.

I remember my time with the signalmen with great affection. They were a wonderful bunch. Men like John Haddow, the relief man for the Coatbridge area. Some boxes worked 8-4, 4-12, and 12-8, while others preferred 6-2, 2-10, and 10-6. John Haddow lived at Stirling and if I booked him on a 4-12 turn, for example, he couldn't get home that night. Not that he ever complained. He just spent the night in the bothy at Coatbridge Station and caught the first train to Stirling in the morning. Same thing with the 6-2 turn. He would come through with the last train the night before and stay in the bothy till starting time. Not surprisingly, I tried to give John turns where he could get back home the same day he came out but one day he came on the phone to say:

"Ah think you're trying to accommodate me on the shifts, Jimmy."

"What do you mean, John," I asked.

"Well, ah always seem tae be gettin' turns tae suit my train times," he said.

"Ah well, John," I joked,

"That's just the way the cookie crumbles, isn't it...?"

"Well ah don't want ye tae dae onythin' like that," said John.

"Ah widny like the ither signalmen tae think ah wis gettin' favours frae the timekeeper."

Another signalman of fond memory is wee Bobby Sutherland, a Special Class Relief Signalman who covered the Buchanan Street section. A small man, he had acquired an inspector's hat to increase his stature but he had no need to do anything like that to impress me. He was at the top of his particular tree and there was no signal box in the St Rollox Control area — or any other area for that matter — that he was not prepared to enter and work at once, sight unseen.

I blundered when making up the rosters one Saturday and left Sighthill Junction without a man on the back shift. This could have been disastrous since Sighthill controlled everything going in and out of Buchanan Street. With my head office hours, I was off home at mid-day and nowhere around when 2pm came and no sign of a relief for Bobby Sutherland.

To his eternal credit he worked till 10pm without complaint — a sixteen hour turn in a very busy box with nothing to eat other than his early shift piece.

When I came out on Monday morning I realised my mistake at once but when I got Bobby's time-sheet in he had only claimed 6-2 on Saturday. I phoned to thank him for doing the double turn and pointed out that he hadn't claimed for it.

"That's alright, Jimmy, " he said,

"I'll get it back some other time."

As Bobby well knew, there would have been raised eyebrows at his double-turn and I would have been on the carpet, so he worked eight hours for nothing rather than drop me in it. Needless to say, I did make it up to him when things were quiet but I will never forget Bobby Sutherland's kindness to me.

But signalmen are a strange breed. They work on their own and get very lonely at times. I sometimes visited Robroyston West on my way to work and the men there would keep me blethering so long I sometimes had to leg it to catch my train.

At Robroyston East there was an old lad called Terry who used to phone Control regularly during the early days of the Second World War with the information that German parachutists were landing in a nearby field. He got it into his head that the shunters at Robroyston East Yard were trying to poison him and always carried a lemonade bottle full of water from home to make his mid-shift tea rather than rely on water from the tap. One night he was walking home down the line in the black-out when he came to a gradient post. In the dark he thought its metal arms were one of the shunters out to attack him so he determined to get in first by aiming a vicious kick at it. He fractured several bones in his foot and was off work for quite a spell.

Another signalman at Stirling Middle entered in his log at 2am one morning that 'Controller Morrison is underneath the box sending up smoke.' The next time his inspector checked the log he had him taken off somewhere for treatment. But the laugh was that Controller Morrison nearly had to go along with him — he denied it!

I spent most of a year with the signalmen and porters without a harsh word from any of them. Everyone got their holidays when they wanted them and no request from me for extended overtime was ever refused. I met only a few face-to-face but anyone could speak to me at any time through the Control Room and there is no doubt the personal touch worked wonders.

Not The LNER!

Come January 1st 1948 and we were nationalised.

Things carried on as before for a time until we heard, amid feelings of horror and disbelief, that we were to come under the hated LNER!

One of the first actions of the new authority was to do away with my job and place the signalmen and porters under a timekeeper at Queen Street Control. The new man could not speak to his men by phone and they had no idea who or where he was. Instructions were sent out by telegram and the men were so fed up they got up a petition to have me reinstated but, needless to say, this had no effect, so back into the Control Room I went as assistant on the North Board to Johnnie Walker, with Peter Rintoul as Shift Controller. A much better atmosphere than Andrew Jack's shift but I had got used to the regular 9-5 hours in the Time Office and I chafed a bit at the shift working — particularly since I had taken up saxophone and clarinet as a hobby and was beginning to be offered work playing in dance bands.

But Johnnie Walker was a fine man to work with. Always cheery and never lost his cool no matter how hectic things got. When things did calm down a bit he enlivened the long weary hours on night shift with tales of his father, old Johnnie Walker, a famous driver at Polmadie

Shed.

Old Johnnie Walker was a quiet, taciturn lad, whose main claim to fame was that he always ran to time—never early, never late but always bang on time. How he did it no one knew, for engines had no speedometers in those days and drivers were not supplied with watches.

By way of contrast, another Polmadie driver, Hairy Jock, was a holy terror out on the line. He thrashed his engine and fireman unmercifully, going about the Caledonian Railway with a great display of spinning wheels and plummets of smoke and steam at all times.

One day old Johnnie Walker was booked to work an express from Carlisle to Glasgow. The train was much heavier than usual and a pilot engine was sent to double-head him — none other than Hairy Jock.

"You'll have to lift yer feet the day," cracked Hairy Jock to Johnnie Walker as his fireman coupled on, but Johnnie Walker said nothing, smiling quietly to himself.

Rivalries were forgotten as the two engines strained to lift the heavy train out of Carlisle and up the fearsome Beattock Summit. Every pound of steam was needed and both crews breathed a sigh of relief when they reached the top and gave their panting engines a breather.

But old Johnnie Walker just gave his engine time enough to get its second wind before he opened her up again. Hairy Jock could hardly believe his ears when he heard Walker roaring at his back down the falling gradients through Clydesdale. And then the penny dropped!

Johnnie Walker's engine had modern oil axleboxes on its tender, whereas Hairy Jock's still had old-fashioned grease boxes and, as the train's speed mounted into the eighties, clouds of smoke started to pour from Hairy Jock's tender.

He shook his fist and danced with rage on his footplate but there was really nothing he could do about it and when they got to Carstairs he had to couple off and go to the shed for repairs.

"Never mind," Johnnie Walker smiled in answer to Hairy Jock's furious tirade.

"We'll easy manage without you!"

And so he did, arriving in Glasgow Central neither early or late but ON TIME!

Our boss, the District Controller, old Andra Ford, did not take kindly to the new LNER regime, nor to his immediate superior, a man called Moss.

Mr Moss was a very energetic sort of person, always rushing hither and yon, and he irritated us considerably by dashing into our Control

Room just after eight in the morning when we were sitting down to our meal break asking such ridiculous questions as "Where's Wishaw...?"

One morning he said to Andra Ford:

"I think you and I'll take a walk down the line to Buchanan Street this morning."

"Whatever ye say yersel', Mr Moss," replied Andra agreeably.

"Bit it'll be gey daurk in the tunnel, ye ken..."

We who were earwigging in the background could hardly believe our ears. Imagine! He didn't know there was a tunnel between St Rollox and Buchanan Street!! We couldn't believe it.

Andra Ford was approaching retirement and would soon be well away from it all but he was very gloomy about our prospects under the hated LNER. Sometimes he left his private office to come into the Control Room and stand gazing thoughtfully out across our main line to the LNER shunting yard at Sighthill.

"Whit dae ye think o' that, Broon?" he asked me one day when I joined him at the window.

"That's the L & NB Railway."

I presumed he was making an obtuse reference to the LNER's predecessor, the North British, but I did not contradict him.

It did not pay to contradict old Andra Ford. He came to us from Polmadie Control with a fearsome reputation for taking his walking stick and chasing recalcitrant controllers all round the office so I was always at pains to keep on the right side of him.

"They ca' me 'the Panda', Broon," he went on.

"Whit the hell's a panda...?"

"Nae idea Mr Ford," I assured him nervously.

"Ah've never heard anybody calling ye anything!"

He had a slow, ponderous gait, and I well knew his nickname, which had followed him from Polmadie, but I had no intention of getting in bad with him and maybe being chased round the office with a walking stick.

I had a couple of lieu days holiday to collect but every time I broached the subject with Mr Ford in the Control Room he brushed me aside.

"Nae time for holidays, Broon," he would shout.

"Get oan wi' yer work."

This was all very well and I knew he was joking — or at least I hoped he was joking — but I was determined to get my leave so I cornered him one day in his private office.

"Whit aboot ma holidays, Mr Ford," I said resolutely.

To my astonishment he backed down at once.

"When dae ye want them, Broon," he asked mildly.

"Next week," I blabbered quickly, before he changed his mind.

"Whit ur ye daein' next week...?" he asked.

"Ah'm oan fur Richardson Monday and Tuesday and spare the rest o' the week," I said.

"Ah well, ye might as well tak' the rest o' the week aff, fur a' the good ye are onywye," sighed old Andra wearily.

I still don't know whether he was joking or not but I did take the rest of the week off and I never heard any more about it.

About this time our hours were cut from 48 to 44 a week and to fit in with our shifts it was decided that we should work 48 hours one week and 40 the next, gaining a 'Rest Day' once a fortnight.

To keep things fair a complicated roster was drawn up, so that we got a Monday off one fortnight, a Tuesday the next, and so on, so that we all got a fair turn of the precious Friday or Saturday off.

To someone like Sandy Clark the upheaval in his regular progress round the three shifts was a bit of a nuisance and it wasn't the first time he travelled all the way in from his home in King's Park with his piece under his oxter only to be turned back at the door.

When Johnnie Walker was on his Rest Day it meant I was on my own on the North Board and I quite enjoyed the sense of power this gave me as I decided who would do what at the start of each shift. But I wished with all my heart that Johnnie Walker was standing beside me and not on his Rest Day one morning when I answered the phone from Garnqueen North Signal Box to be told:

"That's the engine o' the ten o' clock failed here!"

The ten o' clock express from Glasgow Buchanan Street to Aberdeen.

The prestige train of the day! I had watched it pass our window just after ten with ten coaches and a near-new LMS 'Black Five', and here it was stalled at Garnqueen North where the line from Buchanan Street joined that coming from the south through Coatbridge.

For a moment I felt like taking to my heels but the panic passed and I set about getting the train moving again.

The only thing I had handy was an Austerity 2-10-0 just passing Coatbridge with a goods train for Stirling. Very small wheels, but he had the power and the all-important vacuum brake. He wouldn't make much speed but at least he would get the train moving again.

So I gave orders for him to leave his train in the sidings at Garnqueen, ditch the dead engine, and get on the front of the ten o'clock. This gave me a breathing space to look around for something faster.

An old Midland 'Compound' 4-4-0 was just arriving at Larbert with a train of empty coaches from Perth, so I told him to clean his fire and get ready to work the ten o'clock from Larbert. The 'Compounds' were good engines in their day but that day was passing rapidly, and this particular engine was well past its best, as the driver told me in no uncertain terms.

"Work the ten o'clock wi' this bunch a' scrap," he howled.

"Ah'll never get up Kinbuck!"

"You let me worry about that," I assured him with a confidence I did not feel.

Actually I had forgotten about the gradient from Stirling to Kinbuck but now I got on to Stirling and told them to get their station pilot ready to bank the ten o'clock as far as Kinbuck. Meantime I had alerted Perth Control to have a fresh engine ready to take the train on to Aberdeen and I felt quite pleased with myself when the battered old 'Compound' ran into Perth with the ten o'clock only forty minutes late.

Not that my work with the failure ended there. I sent the Austerity 2-10-0 back to Garnqueen to pick up his goods train and had another engine sent out to pick up the dead engine and take it back to St Rollox Loco. in disgrace for a post mortem. Then, inevitably, I had to write a full report all about it. Not that this bothered me unduly. I have never found it difficult to string a few words together, unlike some of my colleagues in the Control.

Peerless railwayman as he undoubtedly was, Sandy Clark sometimes had difficulty with his spelling and I well remember one night he asked me how to spell 'week'.

"Week...?" I said "W E E K"

"No' that 'week'", said Sandy.

"Well, W E A K then" I offered.

"Naw," snorted Sandy impatiently.

"The 'week' ye pit in a lamp!"

The men out on the line always knew when Johnnie Walker was on his Rest Day and 'the boy' was in charge and some of them were not slow in trying to take advantage.

One Saturday afternoon I sent a 'Black Five' to Polmaise Colliery near Stirling to pick up a train of coal. When he got there the driver came on the phone to say his train was well up the colliery branch and he was afraid to go for it with his big engine in case he spread the road and came off.

"There's a train of empty bogies (coal wagons) lying there, isn't there?" I said.

"Well, couple on to them, shove them up the branch, couple your train on to the far end, pull it down, ditch the bogies, and get on your way."

"Aye, right," said the driver and that's what happened.

Of course, the driver knew the solution to the problem as well as I did, but it was Saturday afternoon and he would be a mug to pass up the chance of an early louse. No offence taken on either side, but maybe he would know better than to try to put one over on me next time.

Another Saturday afternoon when I was on myself the engine working a local passenger from Larbert to Grangemouth couldn't raise the vacuum on his train. The station pilot that day was a Caley 'Jumbo' in the 57400 range, which told me he was fitted with the vacuum brake, so I told the drivers to exchange footplates and get the passenger away. So far so good, until the driver left with the engine that had the defective vacuum brake ejector came on the phone to say:

"There's nae brake oan this engine... ah suppose ah'd better make for the shed...?"

Now his engine was a Caley 'Bogie', and that class had a Westinghouse air brake on the engine as well as a vacuum brake ejector for working a passenger train.

"You've no vacuum ejector," I replied. "But are you telling me your Westinghouse brake has failed as well...?"

"Er... no... I never thought about that..." said the driver, and went on his way. No harm in trying, of course, but you had to be on your toes at all times.

A Telegram From The Queen!

The Royal Train seldom ventured into our territory, for which we were truly thankful. When it did, the preparations were really something. Two 'Black Fives' on the train for a start, plus other engines in steam at various strategic points, with still others standing by with steam up at all the sheds. Each engine had to have TWO firing shovels because it was not unknown for a fireman's hands to become so slippery with sweat that the shovel went into the firebox along with the coal. When that happened the train had to stop because it is just not possible to throw coal into the firebox with the bare hands fast enough to keep up steam on a passenger train.

Back in the thirties, two Midland 'Compound' 4-4-0s had the job until one morning they couldn't lift the Royal Train from a branch where it had been stabled for the night. The morning was wet and their big 6' 9" drivers just couldn't get a grip. Red faces all round and the 'Black Fives' got the job from then till the end of steam in Scotland.

Stationmasters and inspectors were out all along the route and the train's progress was reported past every signal box to Control using the code word 'Purple'. In earlier days the senior supervisor at Buchanan Street Telegraph Office, Davie Blair, travelled with the train along with a lineman in case of accident when it would be their duty to climb the nearest telegraph pole to get in touch with authority by means of the Morse Code.

Between trips the train was brought into St Rollox Works for checking and kept in the Varnish Shop under guard until it was next needed. The Queen has a chamois leather sleeve on her lavatory seat which is taken off and laundered after every trip. A step up from the cold plastic I have to endure and one I would like to see introduced into my own domestic life, but all references to it have so far fallen on deaf ears.

Back in Queen Victoria's time the precautions were even more severe. A pilot engine was sent out half an hour in front of the Royal Train to explode any bombs that might have been planted and there was at least one occasion when armed sentries lined the Royal route with each man in sight of his neighbour.

Caledonian 123 was earmarked for the pilot job in her heyday and she still carries the headboard to this day in her retirement home at the Glasgow Transport Museum in the Kelvin Hall.

Soon after the end of the Second World War the present Queen and her mother went down to the Tail o' the Bank to see off the original 'Queen Elizabeth' after her wartime service as a troopship. They journeyed to Balmoral afterwards and the Royal Train was stabled for the night on the Denny branch — bang in the middle of my patch.

Things were quiet till about 2am when a cultured English voice came on the phone from Larbert South.

"This is Major So-and-So," said the voice.

"Equerry to Her Majesty... take a telegram, please..."

A telegram...?

It was more like a small book!

It was the usual effusive message of goodwill to the ship and all who sail in her, etc., and I soon got it down on to a piece of scrap paper. But what was I going to do with it now — stuck in an old wooden cattle shed they called a Control Office miles from anywhere?

I tried the Telegraph Office at Buchanan Street but here my reputation as a joker did me no good at all.

"Listen, Norrie," I said to old Norrie Easton when he eventually answered the phone. Things were quiet at night in the Telegraph Office and he sounded as if I'd wakenend him from a deep sleep.

"I've a telegram here frae the Queen."

"Away you and **** yersel'" replied Norrie, slamming his phone down. It took quite a few attempts before I finally convinced him I was serious.

"Well, whit dae ye expect us tae dae wi' it...?" he grumbled eventually.

I could see his point. They had a cash box and stamps to enable them to take in telegrams from the public which they sent up their pneumatic tube to the Post Office. But this marathon far exceeded the value of the stamps they had on hand. And who was going to put the money in the box?

I suggested he send the telegram up the tube without stamps but Norrie wasn't too keen on that idea.

"Get the Post Office on the line and see what they say," I said.

We roused someone at George Square but he wasn't very helpful either, going on about rules and regulations.

I was beginning to get a bit worried by this time. What was the penalty for not carrying out a Royal command? The Tower of London? Beheading...? After a bit more argy-bargy I took a decision.

"Charge it up to Buckingham Palace," I said.

"On whose authority...?" the man from the Post Office wanted to know.

"Mine," I said.

"Jimmy Brown of the LMS Railway."

I never heard any more about it.

My friend Bob Gray had a lot more to do with the Royal Train than I ever had. Like me, he moved to the Control side of things after the war, becoming an Inspector, among other things, before going on to end his career as Area Manager at Ayr.

Bob was the archetypal railwayman. Completely dedicated to his work and liable to be found out on the line at all hours whether he was being paid for it or not. Even in our boyhood days in Buchanan Street Telegraph Office he would spend his precious ten-minute break down in the Enquiry Office serving the public.

Like most of us he had a nickname — 'Black Bob' after his thatch of thick black hair.

Going along the line checking the signal boxes one day, Bob entered Cardowan box only to find the signalman busy handling a passing train. The phone from the last box he'd visited was ringing so Bob answered it himself.

"Watch yersel'" cautioned the voice at the other end in a hoarse whisper.

"Black Bob's makin' in your direction."

"The signalman's busy at the moment but I'll give him your message as soon as he's free," replied Bob crisply.

"Oh... who's speakin'" asked the voice at the other end, puzzled.

"Black Bob," said Bob Gray, hanging the phone up.

The first time the Royal Train was hauled by a diesel locomotive in Scotland Bob had charge of it coming up through Fife making for Aberdeen with the Duke of Edinburgh en route for Balmoral.

To his horror the train ground to a halt somewhere in the middle of nowhere with a complete engine failure. It was early in the morning and HRH was still fast asleep so Bob set out across a newly-ploughed field to where he could see a road. He was in luck when the first car to come along the road turned out to be a police car. Stopping the car, he explained his predicament but, not surprisingly, like me with Norrie Easton on that other Royal occasion, he had some difficulty convincing the officers he was genuine.

They did believe him in the end and radioed his request for urgent assistance to the railway authorities at Dundee. Bob returned to the train to find the Duke awake with his head out the window demanding to know what was going on. He explained the position, which displeased HRH so much he ordered Bob to arrange for a Land Rover to pick him up at Dundee and take him from there direct to Balmoral. Bob did as ordered via the friendly police car and soon a relief engine appeared to take them on to Dundee.

Bob was in a bit of a sweat, for there had been no time to organise security at Dundee but HRH thought nothing of it and, so far as Bob could see, he quite enjoyed mingling with the office typists and other commuters as they went through the ticket barriers at Dundee Tay Bridge Station.

Later in his career Bob was Operating Assistant to the Area Manager at Aberdeen. The Area Manager himself always turned out personally for the Queen and the Duke but he left the lesser Royals for Bob to handle. One night he was supervising the Duke and Duchess of Kent's children — then quite young — for a spell. To amuse them, he took them over to the bookstall to buy them a comic. This was a novel experience for the young Royals and they were taking more time than usual to make up their minds, which seemed to irritate the elderly lady behind the counter somewhat.

"Hurry up," she chivied the Royal children.

"An' no keep yer faither waitin'!"

Dinna Sprain Yer Ankle Again!

After a couple of years in the Control I realised I would have to do something about the conflicting claims on my time.

I was making good progress with my other interest in life — music — and had joined a band. We were being offered regular engagements and while Peter Rintoul and Johnnie Walker were very good at allowing me to come in late on night shift and letting me away early on back shift the time was coming when I would have to choose.

"There's some jobs going over in the Stores Department," my friend Jack Lavery told me one day.

Jack was a few years older than me and I regarded him as the big brother I never had. A neat, typical railway clerk, Jack worked in the Time Office attached to the Control, making up the paybills. We were paid fortnightly in pound notes, in line with a local agreement, and for some of the men on shifts this could add to fifteen or sixteen pounds, if they had a night shift or a Sunday in it. Jack had a peculiar sense of humour and he took a great delight in extracting any dirty pound notes from the bundle and putting them into the pay packets of people he didn't like. If there were no dirty pound notes supplied, Jack would dirty some in the fireplace. Bent pennies were also kept for his enemies and if there weren't any in the change he would get a hammer and bend some.

When I was Signalmen's Timekeeper I used to ride shotgun with Jack when he took the tramcar down to the bank in Castle Street to collect the pay, until one day a band of criminals broke into St Rollox Station, assaulted the stationmaster, and made off with the payroll in a Paterson's taxi. The haul was considerable since, although St Rollox itself was only a small wayside station, it paid the wages of the men in the many yards dotted around. When Jack heard about the robbery he nearly had a canary.

"There we are," he said,

"Goin' doon tae that bank every second Thursday in the tramcaur an' we could be held up tae. This is nae bliddy good. We'll need tae get a

34

taxi!"

Jack Lavery made no secret of the fact that he was a born coward. Called up to the RAF during the war, he was aghast when they made him an armourer. It was their own fault, he said, that he shot up the drome several times and nearly killed the sergeant. Sent out to service an aircraft with a special highly-secret bomb on board, Jack pressed the wrong button and dropped the bomb onto the tarmac where it lay ticking ominously. Fortunately it didn't go off but Jack gave his superiors something to think about that day.

On D-Day, June 6th, 1944, Jack congratulated himself on being based at Invergordon, safely out of the way. He was horror-struck when, on that very morning, his squad got urgent orders to fly down to Dover straight away. He had never flown in his life and here he was going down to where he was sure there must be many German aircraft flying about trying to stop the invasion.

There was nothing for it but to draw his parachute and get aboard, but in his nervousness he picked up his chute by the ripcord, causing it to fly open. There was no time to get another and Jack sat there all the way down to Dover, the only man without a parachute, figuring out his chances of grabbing somebody else's chute if the worst came to the worst.

Having survived all that, Jack Lavery did not see why he should take any risks with the St Rollox Control paybill, so into Andra Ford's private office he went, with me at his heels.

"Lissen Mr Ford," said Jack.

"We want a taxi tae go fur the wages!"

It was a strange thing about Andra Ford. Out in the Control Room he was all threats and bluster yet when you cornered him in his den, he was a pussy cat after all — as I found out earlier over the matter of my two days' holiday.

"Aw right, Jack," said Andra wearily.

"If you want a taxi get a taxi!"

Back out to the Control Room we went to phone a taxi.

Now Patersons' were the biggest taxi firm in Glasgow and it was natural that Jack should try them first, even if one of their vehicles had been involved in the St Rollox Station robbery.

I stood by and when Jock got through and asked for a cab the party at the other end must have said all the taxis were out.

"Oh they're aw oot, ur they...?" grunted Jack sourly.

"Aw oot robbin' stations, ah suppose...?"

The author's father, Mr William Brown, with a pair of Caledonian Railway horses at Gushetfaulds goods station, Glasgow, circa 1914.

Caley 'Jumbo' 17412 takes her ease at St Rollox Loco.   (Keith Jones collection)

St Rollox Works' clerks Jack Lavery (left) and Frank Kennedy enjoy a golf outing to Gleneagles circa 1938.

The 10.00am Glasgow Buchanan Street to Aberdeen passing St Rollox station in 1948. All coaches are in the then-new BR crimson and cream livery except for the front two. These are still in LMS colours and were probably added as an afterthought to the train.
The loco is a brand-new 'Black Five'.

A local loco at Stirling. No 14356, former Caledonian 4-4-0. (Keith Jones collection)

Glasgow St Rollox Control, 1948.
From left — back row: *Willie McLauchlan (Class 5 Asst Controller), Alan Manson (Asst Controller L&D), Archie Clark (Plant Controller), Jimmy Brown (Asst Controller North).* Front row: *Peter Rintoul (Shift Controller), Andrew Ford (District Controller), Jimmy Peden (Controller L&D), Johnnie Walker (Controller North). The photograph was taken outside the Control Office on St Rollox cattle bank.*

Buchanan Street telegraph clerks George Erskine and the author met by accident at Durban while serving in the Royal Navy in 1944.

Works manager at Crewe, Andy Hume, the man who earlier had put life back into Caledonian number 123.

BR 'Black Five' number 73146 with Caprotti valve gear at St Rollox Loco Sheds in 1957. The author's brother, driver Frank Brown is looking out of the loco window.

In the end we secured a local taxi and the railway policeman for the area and his dog and, thus protected, fetched up the money from the bank in Castle Street.

"You know," said Jack later, as he sorted out the dirty pound notes for his enemies,

"We're right stupid. There we were in the middle o' Springburn Road wi' aw that protection an' naebuddy wid've looked near us — an' here we are up here where onybuddy could come in that door therr an' away wi' the money.

He was right, too.

The control building sat by itself at the end of the cattle bank, with the controllers at one end, and Jack and I sitting in a small office at the other end.

A few minutes later I excused myself on the grounds that I had to go to the toilet.

But I didn't go to the toilet. I rounded up a few of the lads from the Control Room, masked them with green guards' flags and armed them with brake sticks, and burst in on Jack demanding the money.

Poor Jack. The shock he got was even worse than his D-Day adventure but he did see the joke eventually after we'd brought him round.

And this was what Jack was advising me to give up?

A congenial job among lads who had become my friends, with the possible exception of Andrew Jack, that is. I knew nothing at all about the Stores Department other than that there were some bonny lassies working there. When I joined the Navy, the girls in the Stores Department organised themselves into a roster and one of them wrote to me each day. This lasted for a while but in my case absence did not make the heart grow fonder and they gradually dropped out one by one.

What brought matters to a head was the marriage of my brother, Bill. I was the best man, MC and bandleader for the reception afterwards. I should have been on early shift that week but at the last minute Andra Ford switched me on to late turn. He would have let me off the day of the wedding, I know, but I really needed to be free all week to attend to my many duties.

What to do...?

On night shift the week before I had received an ankle injury playing football — a pastime we indulged in during quiet spells, charging up and down the Control Room after a paper ball. The injury wasn't too bad, really, but I went to the doctor and he gave me a sick-line for the week.

It was the only time I've ever done anything like that — and I'm not very proud of myself even yet — but I thought I'd gotten away with it until one day old Andra Ford came up to stand beside me as I warmed my nether regions at the fire.

"See an' no' be blawin' that hooter o' yours ower hard the night," he advised.

"An mebbe sprainin' yer ankle again!"

I might have known. You couldn't fool old Andra Ford that easy!

Next day I wrote out a formal application for a transfer to the Stores Department, and within a matter of weeks I had been interviewed and accepted.

I was sad to leave the Control but I was still a railwayman and I looked forward to my new duties with some anticipation.

Stores Stories

When I moved over to the former LMS Stores Department in Charles Street, about the only things I knew about that organisation was that all requisitions had to be made out in quintuplicate and whatever we needed to run the trains couldn't be got. Guards' handlamps, engine and tail lamps, shunting poles, brake sticks — I'd lost count of the times Andra Ford had to phone across to the General Stores in desperation while men stood waiting in St Rollox Top Yard for the essential tools of their trade.

One thing I was pleased to note at once — the former LMS had come out top dog after nationalisation, unlike the Operating side, where LNER men ruled. Top man was a former Army major, Mr C R Atkins, a thorough gentleman in every respect, unlike some of his right-hand men. As Stores Officer, he had a Divisional Storekeeper at St Rollox and one at Cowlairs to look after the former LMS and LNE sections of the railway.

The workshops at St Rollox and Cowlairs had to be kept supplied, as had all the outstations and depots, and I was very impressed with the extent of the General Stores under Bob Pringle, who had lost a leg in the First World War. Due to some bureaucratic mix-up, Bob had been recorded as having been killed, and his name is on the Memorial Plaque at Glasgow Central. Bob thought this was hilarious and often dragged friends down to see it. Under Bob Pringle, a squad of 48 storemen made up parcels and depatched them to every part of the system by passenger train.

At one time there was a Stores Train that loaded up with brooms, lamps, oil, soap, toilet paper and the hundred and one things needed to run a railway before setting out along the line. Supplies were off-loaded at each signal box, station and yard as they went along and when night came they parked themselves in a siding and slept in the dormitory van provided. The Stores Train had been abolished by the time I joined in 1949 but the vans still stood in the Stores Yard.

Why they did away with the Stores Train I never did find out, although there were stories about how the men sometimes sold off some of their goods to the local population in return for beer money. Certainly things like matches were much sought after.

The railways had their own special safety match called Clock Brand, and Bob Pringle, who smoked a pipe, read the riot act one day after he came off a bus in Royston Road and bought a box of his own matches in the local paper shop.

But the range of things stocked in the General Stores was mind-boggling. Bikes, blankets, briefcases, ladies sanitary towels, clocks, watches — even things like darts, dominoes and ludo. We supplied the Clyde steamers and camping coaches, so that practically every domestic item could be found in the General Stores.

High value items like chamois leathers, torches and clocks were kept in a special section called 'Woolworths'. But this had only a standard BR padlock securing it and the men on the night shift spent much of their time trying out all the keys in stock until they got one to fit. We knew at once when this happened, as our stock of chamois leathers dropped dramatically but all we could do was try another lock from stock, and hope for the best.

An area was set aside as a sample room where a specimen of everything commonly stocked could be inspected by suppliers. One of these was a sample cake of toilet soap with the initials 'LMS' indented into it. This had been made of wood in the Joiners' Shop many years before but now, of course, it had to be replaced by a new sample reading 'BR SC.REG.' and the old wooden cake of soap was to be thrown out. I saw the chance for some fun and put it in the office washroom for a laugh. Once the joke's potential had been exhausted in the Stores Department I took it over one lunchtime to my old stamping ground, St Rollox Control, and left it in the sink there.

The early shift was coming to an end, and who should go through to wash his hands but the dreaded Andrew Jack. I watched with some trepidation till there was a string of oaths from the wash room and Andrew Jack appeared, to throw the wooden cake of soap the length of the Control Room. The rest of the shift looked startled, while I slipped quietly away and did not visit St Rollox Control again for some time.

After many years of working shifts I relished my new Head Office hours of nine to five, Monday to Friday, and nine to twelve noon on Saturdays. I set to, mastering the intricacies of contracts, invoices, advice notes, demand notes and all the systems then in use for keeping the railway running smoothly so far as its material needs were concerned. Jack Lavery had advised me well about the jobs that were going and opportunities for advancement were much improved.

With nationalisation the Stores Department had expanded and I was surprised to find men of my own age with only eighteen months service holding down Temporary Grade Four posts. I had been Temporary Grade Four in the Control but had to revert to Grade Five on transfer. But I had eleven years service and had sat the difficult age 18 examination to get on the staff. Post war, the railways had to lower their standards and these lads had come in from the street to Temporary Grade Four posts practically overnight. I made it clear to those in charge that I would expect my seniority to be taken into account when permanent appointments were made but this did not happen at first and I had to involve my trade union, the Railway Clerks' Association, before matters were ironed out to my satisfaction.

On the Operating side, we were very much a family and, while we were all ambitious to a greater or lesser degree, there was a sense of the fitness of things in taking your turn for promotion — all things being equal. Not so in the Stores Department, I regret to say.

Mr Atkins' right hand man was a rogue who saw to it that only his cronies got the plum jobs, even cooking the staff records to gain his ends, as we found out years after his death.

But I could look after myself in that regard and for the next ten years I saw to it that, while I did not actually jump the queue promotion-wise, neither did anyone else take advantage of me.

Steam 123

I mastered my work in the Stores Department but at heart I was still an Operating man and at lunch times I used to visited the Graveyard at St Rollox to say farewell to old friends lying there awaiting the breakers' torch — 'Dunalistairs', 'Jumbos', Highland 'Castles' and 'Clans' and the odd G&SW loco that had survived through LMS days. Sad to see them standing silently there when I could remember watching from the embankment at the back of my parents' home at Robroyston as they stormed proudly out of Buchanan Street with trains full of happy holiday-makers.

Two old engines that had escaped the breaker were Caledonian 123 and Highland 103, the 'Jones Goods', which sat in the Varnish Shop restored to Caledonian blue and Highland yellow.

Caledonian 123 was a celebrated engine that had taken part in the great Railway Races of 1888 when she covered the Caledonian section from Carlisle to Edinburgh. Built in 1886 by the NB Loco Co — or Neilson Reid as it then was — in the record time of six weeks for the Edinburgh Exhibition of that year, she was subsequently sold to the Caley. Like the best glamour girls of fiction, there was something mysterious about her. To look at, she is unmistakably Drummond yet the Hydepark company always insisted she was their idea.

Her wheel arrangement of 4-2-2 was then on the way out and she was the only one of her type on the Caley books. In days when engines were being rostered to get the maximum out of them, she just did not fit in. So she was kept on odd jobs like the Royal Train Pilot or for working the Officers' Special. In later years she was kept at Perth for working local trains to Dundee and Forfar and there was a legend about her occasional appearance at St Rollox in those days.

In the thirties a great cry got up to load engines to their limit. A load book was produced and records were scrutinised to ensure that no engine ever ventured out on the line with less than her full load — 30 of goods, or the equivalent for a Caley 'Jumbo', for instance.

One of the Shift Controllers, Jack Harding, was red hot on this and the lads on his shift had some fun watching his reactions when Caledonian 123 turned up at St Rollox Top Yard for a train back to Perth after a special run through with a van of fish. Under the LMS engine numbering system, 123 was lumped together with the other Caledonian passenger engines under the 14000 classification — 14010 she was, and they even committed the ultimate atrocity of painting her in Midland Red! — so Jack would naturally expect her to take around 30 of goods like the other Caledonian passenger engines when working goods. He nearly had a fit when the Top Yard phoned her away as:

"That special frae Perth, Jack — away wi' ten oan..."

"Ten... TEN...!" Jack would roar.

"Ur ye aff yer heid...!"

Explanations would follow and Jack's blood pressure would subside as he settled back into his chair muttering:

"Oh, its that thing again, is it...?"

I visited Caledonian 123 and Highland 103 regularly as they stood silently in the Varnish Shop and could hardly believe it when I heard on the grapevine that there was a chance she might be put back into steam again.

The rumour was true. General Manager James Ness was a real railwayman and with the support of the Stephenson Locomotive Society the project went ahead under Andy Hume, one of the younger foreman in the Caley.

Born in the Parliamentary Road in the Townhead district of Glasgow, Andy served his time in the Caley and when he was appointed a foreman in the Erecting Shop in 1954 he was the youngest man ever to hold such a position. He selected his men carefully and set about the task of bringing 123 back to life. She had been stripped of many of her small, removeable fittings over the years but the original drawings were still available and gradually Andy and his men put everything back together again.

Over the restoration period Andy had the mixed benefit of advice from a succession of visitors and enthusiasts, mainly members of the Stephenson Locomotive Society anxious to make sure they were getting their money's worth, for the SLS were contributing generously towards the cost of the work.

But he worked on steadily with only a few scares — like when they discovered 123's great drivers had cracks in their spokes. For a time it looked like the whole thing might have to be abandoned until it was realised that crack-detecting machinery was of comparatively recent invention and the cracks in her 7' drivers had probably been there all her life. Permission to proceed was finally given provided the spokes were checked every three months to make sure they hadn't got any worse.

A bonus to the project were the two Caledonian coaches rescued from the scrapheap and painted in the chocolate and cream of the Caledonian Railway. Mixing Caledonian chocolate and cream presented no difficulty to the Paint Shop but it was a different thing when it came to Caley Blue.

No specification exists for Caley Blue. The exact shade was discovered by accident when a locomotive was being hurried out to traffic and not enough of the original Prussian Blue was available. Rather than hold the engine up, the foreman painter diluted what he had with white and the Caley directors were so pleased with the result, they decreed that the new shade should become standard. But no record had been left as to precisely how much white to add to the blue and railwaymen who

45

could remember what Caley Blue looked like were getting pretty thin on the ground.

Andy Hume rounded up a few retired grey-beards in Springburn and brought them back to the Caley, but the veterans couldn't agree among themselves, and what you see 123 in nowadays represents an amalgum of various opinions and the evidence of old paintings of Caley engines.

At last the great day arrived when Caledonian 123 was pulled out of the Erecting Shop and parked in the Steaming Shed, and it seemed almost a desecration when the words 'Steam 123' were chalked on her tender as an instruction to the steaming squad.

All who could wangle away from their post were present that day when the veteran driver allocated to the job finally opened her throttle.

After what seemed an age the great driving wheels moved slowly and then spun round furiously as she slipped and roared joyously in her chimney with the thrill of being alive again.

Andy Hume and the old driver set out up Germiston High Bank to the main line to let 123 stretch her legs while the rest of us stood around beaming at the success of our labours. At last we spotted the flash of blue in the distance as she backed down the High Bank and Andy Hume stepped down from the footplate looking very pleased with himself.

"Perfect," he pronounced,

"We had her over eighty!"

Now we all knew that 123 had no speedometer and even if she hadn't made eighty, we all wanted her to, and were quite prepared to take Andy's word for it. All except the Works Manager, that is.

"Nonsense!" he said.

"I'll take her out tomorrow to see for myself."

Andy Hume was annoyed at having his word doubted. He was a man of considerable ability — as witness his subsequent career which took him to Inverurie as Locomotive Repairs Engineer and on to the managerships of Eastleigh and Derby Locomotive Works, ending with his appointment as Works Manager at Crewe, then the biggest locomotive works in Europe.

So Andy took the old driver to one side.

"See that ******* o' a Works Manager...?" he said.

"He says you're a ******* liar!"

"Whit...?"

"Aye, he says you never hid 123 up tae eighty at a'. He says he's goin' oot himsel' tomorrow tae see whit she can dae!"

"Is he...?" said the old driver.

"Right... ah'll show him!"

What speed 123 reached on the second day will never be known but it is a fact that the Works Manager descended from the footplate after his run white-faced and trembling, and any mention of 123 in his company from then on put him in a very bad mood indeed.

The success of 123 and her two Caledonian coaches on enthusiasts' specials secured us the go-ahead to restore Highland 103 to full working order and rescue Great North of Scotland Number 49 'Gordon Highlander' and North British Number 256 'Glen Douglas' from the scrap heap.

Each was restored to its company colours, although some poetic licence was taken in the case of 'Gordon Highlander'. The GNSR had switched to black before she came on the scene but we put her into their original GNSR green. While Highland 103 holds the distinction of being the first 4-6-0 to be built in Britain, she was primarily a goods engine and, like 'Glen Douglas' and 'The Sodger' as 'Gordon Highlander' was known, had no great claim to fame beyond a steady record of good work well done. Caledonian 123 was undoubtedly the most glamorous of the quartet and she even ventured as far away as London to show off her beauty to English enthusiasts.

The veteran quartet lived happily together at Dawsholm Shed in the Maryhill district of Glasgow, venturing out singly, or in pairs, to make appearances at events in various parts of Scotland until the mid-1960s when they were moved to the new Glasgow Transport Museum.

Diesel Days

Change was in the air as the decade of the fifties drew to a close. Steam was on the way out and orders were being placed for a variety of diesel locomotives. English Electric 0-6-0 shunters were already commonplace in shunting yards, although they still had a fireman with them in line with union agreements.

The first thing to strike me was the variety of different types being ordered. This was going to be a nightmare from a spares point of view, especially after the gospel of standardisation that had been preached since 1923 where the LMS-designed locos all had various common standard parts in their builds. Indeed the rush to standardisation had seen many bonny engines consigned to the Graveyard at St Rollox years ahead of their time, especially the former Glasgow and South Western stud which had been replaced by LMS Class 2P 4-4-0s of indifferent performance which often stalled on the steeper gradients like the road up from Fairlie Pier.

But ours not to reason why.

Diesel Stores were set up at Cowlairs and St Rollox as we set about the apparently endless task of introducing stocks of items that looked more like motor car spares than parts of machines destined to work on the iron road.

Another change was the amalgamation of the separate Stores Departments at St Rollox and Cowlairs under a new Supplies and Contracts Manager, Mr H Cheetham, in the former G & SW offices at St Enoch Station in Glasgow. Depot Storekeepers with small staffs were left at both works but the bulk of the ordering for the Scottish Region of British Railways was now done at St Enoch.

Changes in musical tastes caused me to abandon my band activities and I concentrated more on my railway career, working my way steadily up the promotion ladder until I was appointed Class 1 Inspector for Planning and Productivity under the St Enoch reorganisation.

I had made friends among my Stores Department colleagues but I made no attempt to hide my contempt for those among us who regarded working on the railway solely as a career with no regard to the tradition of the thing. I always felt it was an honour to be a railwayman and, if necessary, I was quite prepared to work for nothing if it was the only way to keep things running. But it has to be said that there were some who socialised outside office hours while plotting to get their hands on the levers of power without regard to the justifiable hopes and aspirations of their workmates.

My Operating experience came in handy when identifying the various types of engines requiring spares. I had only to hear an engine number to recite at once its class, wheel arrangement, where it was built, what its power classification and load was, and so on. Where I came from, everyone knew this, and it irked me to see these late-comers aiming to take over when they were so woefully ignorant.

As regards my new appointment, so far as I could see I was just a trouble-shooter and if everything was running according to plan I had no job to do. More than once my telegraph experience came in handy when the switchboard operator failed to turn up and on these occasions I sometimes reflected that I must have been the highest paid switchboard operator on British Railways.

Things did go wrong, of course, like the time the Stock Verifiers reported that the spare lock gates at the Grangemouth end of the Forth & Clyde Canal could not be found. How these came to be in railway stock beats me — maybe BR owned Grangemouth Harbour...? but I caught the first train there only to find out that the spare lock gates were there all right — only they had become so overgrown with weeds that the verifiers couldn't see them — or said they couldn't see them. I suspect it was a case of inter-departmental rivalry.

Another day Cowlairs Wagon Shop was said to be at a standstill for lack of bolts. I grabbed the first tram and made for the store.

"Ah don't know whit happened, Mr Brown," said the worried storeman.

"We had plenty yesterday but the bin's empty noo".

Whatever job you hold down in this life, there is no substitute for experience, and my experience of Cowlairs Wagon Shop warned me they were up to something.

Acting on a hunch, I checked the scrap bins and there, sure enough, were piles of brand-new bolts that had been in stores stock yesterday. As I suspected, the Wagon Shop had been criticised for lack of production and were looking round for an alibi. Like the Israelites in bondage in Egypt who complained they couldn't make bricks without straw, the favourite excuse for not getting on with it is still lack of materials, and when there was no such excuse handy Cowlairs Wagon Shop created one by drawing out our bolt stock and throwing it on the scrap heap.

But after I'd finished with them that day, that was one excuse they didn't try again!

Another job that came my way arose through the introduction of diesels into St Enoch. The station had a lovely big arch modelled on London St Pancras, obviously an ideal roosting place for pigeons and the like. In steam days the blast from the engines' exhausts kept the arch clear but once they had largely gone the birds came in and their droppings caused complaints from passengers since the platform surface became very slippery in wet weather. The problem landed on my desk.

We stocked a chemical preparation in the General Stores at St Rollox for use in the lavatories of camping coaches and I figured if it dissolved the human effort, it might be equally effective on bird droppings, so I ordered this to be spread on the platforms at St Enoch. It worked a treat. Too well, in fact, for not only did it dissolve the birds' droppings, it dissolved the passengers' shoes as well!

Fortunately for me, perhaps, I moved on at this time although I did hear that my successor solved the problem rather neatly by draping wire netting over the arch-ends. For some reason the birds would not dip beneath the netting to reach the station. I would never have thought of that.

Promotion-wise I was not too happy at this time. A couple of that clique I mentioned had manoeuvred themselves slightly in front of me in the race to the top and when I did not get a post I had occupied without complaint for six months, I decided it was time to sling my hook from the Supplies & Contracts Department at St Enoch. A job in the next grade up was advertised down at London Liverpool Street so I put in an application and promptly forgot all about it. Months later I got a shock when our staff office told me to report to Liverpool Street next day for interview.

I had cooled down by this time and didn't really want to shift from Glasgow, so on the way down to London I resolved to talk my way out of the job, since it was bad form to apply for a job and then change your mind.

But my plan misfired. My tactic of disagreeing with the panel a lot, and treating them with much less than the usual respect, had the opposite effect and they were on the phone to St Enoch that afternoon declaring I was the man for them and wanting to know how soon I could be released.

When I checked in next morning Mr Cheetham sent for me and demanded to know what was going on. Apparently he hadn't been told of my original application.

"It's quite simple, Mr Cheetham," I said.

"If you're going to promote deadheads before an experienced railwayman like myself, then its time I wasn't here..."

"But you don't know what plans I've got for you," he replied.

"That's as may be," I said.

"But you could walk out of here tonight straight under the nearest bus and a fat lot of good your plans would do me then. But withdraw my application. I was quite ready to go till you sent for me but now I don't know what to think."

"But they'll blame me for talking you out of going," said Mr Cheetham.

"Well, haven't you done just that...?" I replied, concluding the interview. Actually, I had rather put Mr Cheetham on the spot and soon after I was sent to St Rollox as Acting Assistant Depot Storekeeper. I left St Enoch for the last time in January, 1962.

I haven't many happy memories of St Enoch but I did relish coming into contact with my old pals, the steam engines again. Our office was on Number One platform, and an express to Leeds left there just after nine each morning. Motive power at this time was usually a Gresley A3 assisted by an ex-LMS 2P 4-4-0, working home as far as Kilmarnock. There is a sharp curve out of Platform One at St Enoch and the two engines gave a spectacular show of smoke and steam as they slipped now and then.

These old engines did much of the work on the expresses between London St Pancras and St Enoch and I noticed that the loco working in each morning with the overnight sleeper worked back with the four o'clock in the afternoon from Platform One. Gresley 'Pacifics' make a peculiar singing noise like a kettle coming to the boil and when I heard an engine backing down on its train in the afternoon I used to say to one of the office juniors:

"That sounds like my friend engine number so-and-so. Kindly go out and check if I'm right." The platform couldn't be viewed from our office but I'd made a mental note of that morning's engine number and, of course, I was always right. The young lads were baffled and I refused to enlighten them as to how it was done, remarking merely that I knew all the steam engines by their first names. If nothing else, it added to my growing reputation for eccentricity.

During my time at St Enoch our chairman, Sir Brian Robertson, retired. His replacement was Dr Richard Beeching, an industrialist from ICI. Two things bothered me about this appointment. First, his salary was quoted at £25,000 against the £12,000 Sir Brian had been getting. Second, he was said to be a crony of Ernest Marples, Transport Minister and road building tycoon.

The railways had been losing money steadily through the fifties, which wasn't surprising when you consider they weren't allowed to raise their charges in line with their costs. The government preferred to keep rates down and to fund the resulting deficit from the exchequer.

Down at a General Railway Course at Illminster in Somerset in early 1959 among a cross-section of railwaymen, we were treated to a lecture from an economist on the need to make the railways pay.

"But how can we make the railways pay...?" we asked.

"We can only do our jobs to the best of our ability — besides, the country cannot do without railways, whether they pay or not."

"Oh yes it can," replied the economist.

"I'll tell you what will happen if the railways don't pay — we'll close you down!"

I remember yet the roar of laughter that greeted such a preposterous suggestion, and in the bar that night we chortled at the naivety of the man. But it was surely a straw in the wind. A portent of things to come, had we but realised it.

Another thing that made me uneasy at that time was a conversation I had with someone higher up about the superiority of the concrete sleeper over the wooden one.

"The concrete sleeper may be more expensive," I pointed out.

"But it will last up to a hundred years."

"Ah," said the higher-up.

"But who's to say we'll still have railways in a hundred years...?"

A pal of Beeching's maybe...?

Back To St Rollox

So back to St Rollox I went once more.

Adam Johnston was Depot Storekeeper and I warmed to him at once when I heard him on the phone to one of the shop foremen who had evidently incurred his displeasure.

"Did ah wish you a Happy new Year..?" asked Adam.

"Well, cancel it!"

Apart from Adam and me, there were two clerks, a typist and an office messenger to look after the General Store at Charles Street and the Loco and Carriage and Wagon Stores in the works. There was also a Sheet Shop tacked on to the General Store where tarpaulin sheets were manufactured and repaired.

The new Number 9 Diesel Store was burgeoning at the end of the Erecting Shop and my duties were mainly concerned with the setting up of the various new stockheads. But in effect I took to do with all aspects of our work and remain grateful to Adam Johnston for adding greatly to my valuable stock of that rare commodity, experience. As Adam used to say:

"The auld dug barks and the young dug learns!"

In return I handled all the correspondence since Adam's gift did not lie in that particular direction.

Spares were being laid down for the Sulzer Type 2s (later Classes 26 and 27), plus the Derby-built Type 2s (later Class 25s) and, much to my disgust, the ill-fated NB Type 2s (later Class 29).

Fifty eight NB Type 2s had been ordered straight off the drawing board at a cost of £70,000 each. Thirty eight were allocated to the Eastern Region and twenty to the former GNSR area based at Kittybrewster in Aberdeen. The Eastern Region engines were delivered first and from the start they were a complete and utter disaster, wreaking havoc with the schedules out of Liverpool Street. It got so bad they had to be withdrawn from service completely.

I heard all this on the grapevine down at St Enoch and my shock-horror may be imagined when I was sent for and told to organise the transfer of all NB Type 2 spares from Stratford Works, London, to St Rollox.

"But why...?" I asked.

"If these engines are no use down there why bring them up here...?"

Sadly, it was the old story about everything good being kept down in England with only the second-hand or second-rate coming to Scotland.

"It's to be near their place of manufacture," was the only explanation I ever got.

So far as I could see, the whole dieselisation programme was fraught with mistakes like this. There were tried and proven designs operating in the USA that would have suited our purposes admirably but political considerations ruled that the great dieselisation cake had to be sliced up between British manufacturers, regardless of any consideration of track record and reliability.

The North British Locomotive Company had a proud record in steam but they left it too late in changing over to diesel. They secured a licence from the German MAN company to build their engines but something was missing. Maybe it was the German know-how built up over the years — maybe it was something to do with the NB men having to work in Metric after many years in Imperial. Who knows...? The theories are many and varied.

My former happy hunting ground, St Rollox Control, was standing empty since the LNER had closed it down and moved the work to Queen Street so I requisitioned it and had the spares laid out for identification in the old Control Room before taking them into Number 9 Store.

It was a big job and I worked largely on my own, pausing only now and then to commune with the spirits of Sandy Clark and Andrew Jack.

Those engines capable of moving under their own 'steam' made it from London to St Rollox themselves but at least one train load had to be hauled north by a steam engine. The sight of a train of diesels being pulled by a steam engine aroused the curiosity of the Press and one of the Sunday papers did a story about it. This caught the attention of the Glasgow papers, and when they came sniffing about there was no lack of people willing to speak up. It really was a scandal and when pointed articles started to appear, management got annoyed and a discreditable witch-hunt ensued.

My penchant for stringing words together coupled with my unfortunate habit of speaking up when anything threatened the well-being of my beloved railway made me a prime suspect, and I was interviewed, with others, by the General Manager, James Ness.

But nothing could be proved against me and the matter was allowed to drop. As it turned out, the NB Type 2 business worked out to my advantage when it came to filling the temporary appointment I was holding at St Rollox. I suspected my chances of landing the permanent appointment were not good, yet when the time came I was confirmed almost as a matter of course.

Why...? Well, if I had been disappointed after holding the job down on a satisfactory basis for eight months I would have had a cast-iron case of victimisation after my interview with Mr Ness. That's my theory, at any rate, and it's strange how one's life-pattern may be decided by such trivialities.

The NB Type 2s were parked in the Varnish Shop till authority decided what to do with them and on my way home each night I used to cut through that way and stand and stare at these attractive looking engines, some of them still in the same pristine condition as they had been turned out from Hydepark.

Once they had enough of them running they tried them out on the three-hour Glasgow — Aberdeen run but breakdowns became almost an everyday occurance, even after they started running them in tandem as a desperate measure. One of them — 6127 — caught fire at Greenloaning and burned out completely so that there were only the cab-ends still standing when she was dumped with the rest in the Varnish Shop.

One day I spotted the original engine — 6100 — shunting over in Sighthill Yard but she was making strange noises even to my un-tutored ear, and, sure enough, I found her esconsed with her sisters in the Varnish Shop a few nights later.

Something had to be done, and what was done resulted in an unexpected Golden Twilight for a batch of Gresley 'Pacifics' otherwise destined for the scrap heap. They were shedded at St Rollox and Ferryhill and until the end of steam they performed valiantly on the three-hour run through Forfar.

Talk of the NB Type 2s was discouraged but I did learn that modifications were to be undertaken to upgrade them from 1100 to 1350bhp and maybe make them more reliable, but this did not work.

Next I heard a plan was afoot to re-engine 19 of them with a Paxman Ventura engine at a cost of £34,000 each. Why 19...? Well, twenty engines were ordered and one was to be kept as a spare.

One of the silent locos over in the Varnish Shop — 6123 — was selected as a protoype and I watched from the window of our office on St Rollox Cattle Bank the first day she was tried out on the 8.25am to Aberdeen.

As I remarked to Adam Johnston at the time, there seemed to be more bodies on the engine than there were in the train!

Beeching's Blues

Dr Beeching was still deliberating his report in 1962 but already changes were afoot as we noticed when strangers started coming on the phone from a place called Castlefields House at Derby telling us they were now in charge. Apparently the 28 main workshops on British Railways were to be separated from their regions and put together under a new management, British Railways Workshops. This put Adam Johnston and me in a queer position. Nominally we were still under the Supplies and Contracts Manager at St Enoch, yet these people down at Derby were beginning to act as if they owned us.

I should explain that the Stores Departments of the former LMS and LNE Railways were always separate and independent entities. No department was allowed to order anything other than through the Stores Department. Apart from discouraging corruption, this enabled British Railways to place massive contracts at good prices for the many items in common use throughout the system. We were the biggest single purchasing organisation in the country and orders from us kept many suppliers going year after year.

Not that corruption was entirely abolished by this regime, I need hardly add. It merely took it to a higher level and occasionally there were cases in the papers of some high-heid-yin doing something he shouldn't.

Next we heard, Mr Cheetham had departed back south whence he came and the Supplies and Contracts Department was to be abolished after only three years' existence. Meantime we were to come under the Works Manager at St Rollox, not something we relished, as the engineering staff were inclined to regard themselves as superior beings and we storekeepers as mere underlings.

Then we heard the number of main workshops on BR was to be cut from 28 to 16 and we waited with some trepidation to see who would be on the death list. Inverurie was a cert to go, we told ourselves at St Rollox, with a confidence we did not feel. After all, it was the smallest, and stuck at the far end of the line.

But when the list came out, Inverurie was spared and Cowlairs condemned. The men at Cowlairs protested mightily and marched down Springburn Road for a demonstration in George Square. Adam Johnston and I watched them go from the bridge over Springburn Road at Inchbelly Crossing, complete with a home-made coffin representing Cowlairs.

"It won't make any difference," said Adam Johnston. And he was right. Even after Beeching brought out his report, and even after he got a kick up the seat of his pants in Edinburgh Waverley Station for daring to show his face in Scotland, nothing made any difference.

But back in 1962 we were still very much in the dark.

I took a run to Aberdeen one day behind one of the Gresley 'Pacifics'. Driver was 'Kuddy' Walker, brother of Johnnie at St Rollox Control, son of the legendary Johnnie Walker, master of Hairy Jock, and dedicated Caley man.

"What do you think of this machine...?" I asked him before we started.

"Nae ******* use!" declared Kuddy emphatically.

"It stoats ye aboot the cab like a cahoochy ba'.... an' they expect ye tae get tae Stirlin' in forty minutes. Nae ******* use!"

"Surely better than a Black Five...?" I suggested maliciously.

"Is it Dick," roared Kuddy — only 'Dick' wasn't the precise epithet he used.

"Ah hid a Black Five wan day last week an' it could leave this thing staunin.'"

Kuddy was reacting as I well knew he would. As a dyed-in-the-wool Caley man, anything to do with the hated NB was anathema to him. But while the older generation still held to their prejudices, we of the younger school were gradually coming round to the idea that we were all railwaymen together. In the event we got to Perth bang on time and I got a cheery wave from Kuddy and his mate as they walked down the platform after being relieved by Ferryhill men.

"How will that dae ye...?" asked Kuddy.

"Fine," I replied, settling back into the cushions of my first class compartment for the rest of the run up to Aberdeen behind the Ferrryhill men.

The three-hour run with eight coaches was well within the capabilities of the old engines, even at that late stage in their career.

Cowlairs had no Assistant Depot Storekeeper so any time that worthy was off I went over to take charge.

At this time the Depot Storekeeper was my old friend from St Enoch, Andrew Kirkland.

Andrew Kirkland served in the Royal Engineers during the Second World War, attaining the rank of sergeant. He landed in France soon after D-Day in 1944, in charge of the Army's stock of spares for their Austerity 2-8-0 and 2-10-0 steam engines and guarded them carefully as the Allied Armies advanced through France and Belgium to Antwerp where he was relieved and sent home for demobilisation.

After his demob leave was up he reported back to Cowlairs Works to resume his railway career, and what do you think was the first thing he saw as he entered the gates in Carlisle Street...? Exactly! The self-same cases of 2-8-0 and 2-10-0 spares he'd left behind in Antwerp. When Andrew was enjoying his leave the Army had been busy selling their locos and spares to the home railways, and here they were waiting for him once more.

But Andrew often had a suspicion that the fates were conspiring against him — like when he handed a suit to a small establishment in Keppochill Road for dry-cleaning. That night the shop was burgled and his suit was stolen. We were at St Enoch at the time in the Productivity and Inspection Section and the rest of us were suitably sympathetic. But then the sly, malicious questions started.

"Not that old suit you were wearing to the office, surely...? Didn't think it would have been worth cleaning...?"

Or: "Was yours the only suit there, then...?"

Or: "Of course, in the dark the burglar wouldn't be able to see that it was an old suit hardly worth stealing, would he...?"

And so on.

I had a curious power over Andrew Kirkland in that I could reduce him to tears of helpless laughter as I told some highly unlikely story about my time in the Royal Naval Patrol Service when we lost one of His Majesty's ships while fishing, or some such.

On the other hand, Andrew was adept at shooting a line himself and most intolerant when anybody else started putting it on a bit.

One of the other lads in the PPI, Dan Rodger, made an excellent straight man and there were a few memorable occasions when we got Andrew really wound up.

Like the time Count Basie and his Orchestra came to Glasgow in the late fifties.

"I see Count Basie's in Glasgow this week..." said Dan for openers.

"Yes... Bill," I replied.

"Oh... Bill... Is that his real name, then...?" asked Dan, rising to the bait magnificently.

"Yes. Bill Basie," I confirmed.

"Of course, only his friends call him Bill."

"Are you a friend of his, then...?" went on Dan, playing a blinder.

"Friend... Am I a friend...?" I replied scornfully.

"Lissen Dan, the first thing Bill Basie does when he hits town is phone me up to fill him in on the jazz scene."

Dan was suitably impressed.

"Has he never asked you tae join his band, Jimmy...? he enquired respectfully.

"It's the travellin', Dan," I sighed sorrowfully.

"The travellin'".

While this was going on Andrew was growing more and more restless as he struggled to get on with his work, but the idea of me playing in the great Count Basie band was really the last straw.

The biro pen was thrown down on the desk, his specs came off and he let fly.

"Fur Pete's sake! Ah've never heard sich a lot o' rubbish in aw ma born days! You playin' in Count Basie's band...? Don't make me laugh!"

And much more of the same.

Dan Rodger and I looked at one another in feigned surprise and amazement, then turned on him.

"Who rattled your cage...? We're having a private conversation here. Kindly mind your own business and do not interfere in things you do not understand."

And then the recriminations would fly back and forth to the immense enjoyment of all present.

At this time Andrew Kirkland was sent up to Inverurie to relieve the Depot Storekeeper, Jimmy Milne. When he returned he told us all about his adventures in that far-away place but I showed only a polite interest, never guessing that Inverurie would play such an important part in my life later on.

He put up at the Banks o' Ury Hotel and the first night after his evening meal he strolled into the bar for a drink. A waitress served him and left him on his own for he was, as yet, the bar's only customer. Standing there by himself he was startled to hear a stream of oaths and threats coming from the lounge bar next door, apparently directed at him for he was the only one there.

Andrew Kirkland was not the sort of man to take this lying down so he went next door to see what was what — only to find his assailant to be a parrot in a cage!

Later that evening he was joined by several convivial local lads and a session developed that lasted well into the night. Next morning he rose with a terrible hangover and promptly checked out and went into private digs for the rest of his stay.

Later on after I took over at Inverurie, Andrew was Supplies Officer at the Western Region's Swindon Works and we still kept in touch despite the distance. I phoned him one day only to hear from his secretary that he was off ill.

"Good," I said.

"I trust it's nothing slight...?"

There was silence at the other end as she digested this.

Then she went on... "I think he's in hospital..."

"Great," I responded.

"If you let me know which ward he's in, I'll send him a 'Get Worse' card..."

Another silence at the Swindon end and I hugged myself with glee as I imagined the Western lass telling her colleagues: "I always thought Mr Brown and Mr Kirkland were friends...?"

So we were — great friends despite Andrew's LNER background — but where I come from in Glasgow you can only insult your friends. Insulting anyone else can have dire results.

The sixteen Supplies Officers exchanged cards at Christmas and I always got mine out in October to uphold Inverurie's reputation as the best wee workshop on the ground. Andrew Kirkland phoned me one day to protest at this.

"You don't like getting your Christmas Card in October, do you, Andrew...?"

"OK, I'll fix that!"

So next year I sent off his Christmas Card in September and to rub his nose in it I added a McGonagall couplet for good measure.

"If there's ever anything you're no' very sure i'
Just lift the phone and ask Inverurie!'"

I never got any more complaints about Christmas Cards.

But when I used to go across to Cowlairs to relieve Andrew Kirkland I sometimes found myself in the slightly ridiculous position of having to write letters to myself. There was a regular flow of correspondence between the two works and I, of course, signed all the letters emanating from St Rollox. It sometimes happened that I would cross to Cowlairs to find letters awaiting my attention that I had signed the night before at St Rollox.

With the on-going reorganisation of BR Workshops as we entered 1963 Andrew Kirkland moved to Swindon as Supplies Officer and I went across to Cowlairs until a permanent appointment was made. Coincidentally this took place on Monday 28th March, 1963, the day Dr Beeching produced his infamous report and twenty five years to the day since I joined the LMS at Buchanan Street back in 1938.

A new Supplies Officer was to be appointed at St Rollox to cater for both Cowlairs and St Rollox but I was in charge at Cowlairs for three months till this job was filled. I was an applicant and well equipped to do the job but I knew I was still in bad odour in certain quarters after the NB Type 2 business and it came as no surprise when I did not get it.

So back to St Rollox I went once more to hear about the great ideas of a new man who had appeared from Batchelor's Peas to take charge of the Stores side of the Workshops Division.

It seemed to me that all the top jobs were going to people who knew nothing at all about railways.

One of the new regime's first ideas was that each workshop should stand on its own feet with its own accountant, supplies chief, and so on. Then all would compete with one another for the work available. Fair enough, I suppose.

But in our world it meant a considerable disruption. From Glasgow being the headquarters of all administration, now separate organisations would have to be set up at St Rollox, Inverurie, Barassie and Townhill, the small wagon works near Dunfermline.

New posts of Works Supplies Assistants (later Supplies Officers) were created and applications invited. I was really quite happy where I was at St Rollox, and never inordinately ambitious, so I expressed little interest in the new appointments until I was told I was to be made redundant and appointed Travelling Inspector for all warehouses between Inverness and Edinburgh. In those days there was still a caring atmosphere on British Railways and no staff man was ever declared redundant without another post being found for him. But my new job meant that I would be away from home all week, so I fell into a trap that had no doubt been well thought out and applied for the Inverurie job, which was a grade higher.

There was no one already at Inverurie with the necessary experience and none of the Glasgow 'blue-eyed boys' were interested since they were all married and did not want to shift. I was still single and no doubt the opportunity was taken to off-load me onto Inverurie, and good riddance after the NB Type 2 fracas.

The interview was a formality. Derby's new Stores Controller, Mr John McLean, the man from Batchelor's Peas, came up from the south. Inverurie's Works Manager, Mr R L Garden, came down from the north, while a survivor from the Supplies and Contracts Department, Mr D Broom, now called a Stores Comptroller, whatever that means, was in the chair.

"So you want to come to Inverurie, do you...?" asked Mr Garden.

"No, I DON'T want to come to Inverurie," I replied in disgust.

"But I will go up there and set up your supplies organisation for you and then move on."

"Fair enough" he said. And that was that.

In my own mind I had decided there was nothing for it but to take the road south, as so many others had done before me.

I was interviewed on Monday, 9th December, 1963, and reported to Inverurie exactly a week later on Monday 16th December.

Our whole operation at St Rollox was being scrapped at the same time so on my last Friday, Adam Johnston and I took our typist, Anna Angus down town for a meal at lunchtime. There was some cash left in our office tea kitty so we bought a half bottle of whisky to have a farewell dram with the clerks, Bill Fisher and Alec O'Connor when we went back up to St Rollox.

But somehow the word got out that we were having a wee bit of a celebration up in the 'Ranch-house' as the old St Rollox Control building was now known and well-wishers from the works started turning up; like Davie Wyllie from the Trimming Shop and Bob Miller from the Carriage Shop. Our half bottle didn't last long and our office messenger, Ronnie Mc Phillie, had to be sent out for further supplies before our party broke up at five o'clock. Adam Johnston was nearing retirement so he wasn't bothered much and the others were being absorbed into the new organisation, but we were all sad at the end of what had been a happy time for us at St Rollox.

No, I Don't Want To Come To Inverurie!

I caught the 8.25am from Buchanan Street that memorable day, travelling north in the company of Alec Munro, then acting Assistant Works Manager at Inverurie, Peter Lamont, Motive Power Superintendent for the North East, and John Barr, who had been locum at Inverurie pending my appointment.

Up front we had Gresley 'Pacific' 60094, 'Colorado' — Ferryhill's fourth standby, according to Peter Lamont who gave us a running commentary on the driver's performance throughout, with remarks like: "He's fairly thrashing her now!" With my sense of the literary I had visions of the driver taking a cat-o-nine-tails to the poor engine.

Peter had a copy of the Working Timetable, which was timed in half-minutes, and he gave top marks to Stonehaven which he said was the smartest station on the line, with a time of only forty seconds from stop to start again that day.

I was naturally a bit gloomy about leaving my safe, secure surroundings in Glasgow for parts unknown, and John Barr tried to cheer me up.

"Don't worry, Jimmy," he said.

"I've fixed you up with good digs — and I've even got a wife for you!"

He was having me on, of course, but there's many a true word spoken in jest. He was referring to the only member of my office staff already in position in Inverurie, my typist, Margaret. We were thrown together eight hours a day and I came to rely on her while I struggled to find my feet in this alien land so it shouldn't surprise anyone that we fell in love and were married only nine months later.

But thoughts of romance were far from my mind when we arrived in Aberdeen that morning. There was no connecting train so we had to travel out to Inverurie in the works lorry which was standing in the station forecourt with its tailboard down. John Barr and Alec Munro gave me a hand up but instead of joining me, as I expected, they jumped up front in the warm beside the driver, Jimmy Hay, leaving me on my own in the draughty back of the lorry.

I had never been this way before and I kept looking out for signs of a railway as Jimmy Hay took the A96 Inverness road. I spotted signals at what I now know to be Bucksburn, but then we shot off into open country and I was left shivering in the back as we trundled through the snowy countryside. There were a couple of false alarms as we sped through Blackburn and Kintore before Jimmy Hay finally dropped us in front of Inverurie Town Hall.

First call was to my digs to meet my landlord and landlady, Mr and Mrs Mearns. Duncan worked in the Boiler Shop at the works and he and his wife had a lovely cottage near Inverurie Station. They made me very welcome and soon became my friends, regarding me as a second son to their own Jimmy, who was rector of Cumbernauld Academy.

62

That night John Barr took me out to show me Inverurie in what turned out to be a bit of a pub crawl. The town was dark and mysterious to me, with the smell of woodsmoke in the air. The shops were shuttered and silent with only Davidson's chipper and the Victoria Cinema and the odd sweetie shop open to cast a blaze of light into the gloom. Our first call was to the Commercial Hotel in North Street, then we strolled as far as the Banks o' Ury Hotel in High Street to let me see the scene of Andrew Kirkland's epic adventure. The night was pleasant for December so we walked on as far as the Bridge Bar in Port Elphinstone before turning back to the Kintore Arms and ending up in the Gordon Arms near our lodgings at Burnbank.

At the station Adam Kerr was in charge with Margaret Robertson and Hilary Young in the booking office and BIll Glennie in the goods office, and several porters, shunters, guards and signalmen to complete the work force.

John Menzies had a bookstall at the station which was still much as it was built in 1903 with James Gregor as the first stationmaster, grandfather of my typist, Margaret.

The station had a private waiting room for the Earl of Kintore, this apparently being a condition of the sale of the land to the Great North of Scotland Railway. A toilet was also provided but here the canny GNSR people had installed a penny-in-the-slot lock, and one day the Earl did not have a penny when he wished to use it. Mr Gregor came speedily to his rescue with a penny and subsequently the Earl presented him with a beautiful silver dish with a new penny for the year — 1907 — set into it surrounded by the inscription: 'A Friend In Need Is A Friend Indeed.'

First impressions were that I liked Inverurie and its people. My men in the Stores were a great bunch and those I met in my everyday work, like John Stronach, Alex Tosh and Andy McRae could not have been nicer.

But I had a sneaking suspicion that my appointment hadn't been all that welcome at the top level. The Works Manager, Mr Garden, would obviously have preferred to appoint one of his own staff, but Mr McLean had vetoed that on the grounds that no-one at Inverurie had the necessary experience. And I had a good idea Mr Broom would have slipped in the poison about my alleged involvement in the NB Type 2 scandal.

Whatever the reason, I felt distinctly unwanted when Garden told me I would have to conform to ordinary working hours, unlike the others

Jimmy Brown, Supplies Officer BR Workshops Inverurie
— master of all he surveys.

'Meldy Meg' and GNSR coaches at Inverurie Works in 1925.

Inverurie Loco Works: the carriage and wagon shops are in the left
background, the canteen and time office are in the foreground, and the
electricians shop is on the right.

Inverurie Works Manager R L Garden (right) presents 45 years service watch to Alan Wood in 1964 (the author is second from the left).

Ex Great Eastern Railway 'B12' at Inverurie after overhaul.

Several of the dreaded NB Type 2s lurk in Inverurie erecting shops.

Operating Assistant Bob Gray (Black Bob) with Miss Rail News at Aberdeen Joint Station in 1965.

Inverurie Loco Works offices in 1969.

Condemned vans being loaded at Inverurie.

Enthusiasts outing at Aberdeen harbour in the sixties.

Works Manager John Stronach blows Inverurie Loco Works horn for the last time — 1205 hours on the 31st December, 1969.

Once a railwayman, always a railwayman — Jimmy Brown sees off fellow rail enthusiast Martin Thorley-Smith at Inverurie station in 1985.

English Electric Type 3 on the 1340 Aberdeen-Inverness at Inverurie in 1986.

from Glasgow who were allowed to travel up on Monday morning. Next I found that the new furniture I had sent on from St Rollox for my new office had been purloined by the personnel office. A few other pinpricks annoyed me until one morning I wheeled the personnel assistant in before the Works Manager and let fly. In the end, matters were smoothed over to my satisfaction and from then on I had no trouble from any of them. It was the old story about the pecking order and, once I had shown my mettle, that was that.

Another small incident made my name with the men in the store.

I was coming up the Stores Bank after lunch in my smart suit, well polished shoes and trilby hat when I came upon one of my men struggling with a sack barrow that had got stuck between a wagon and the bank. Without thinking about it, I threw my weight behind the barrow to extricate it and walked on. But later I heard the word went round like lightning:

"Did ye hear aboot the new mannie...? He's no feart tae get his hands dirty!"

But I had a mammoth task before me. I arrived on the Monday and John Barr left for Glasgow at Thursday lunchtime. My typist, Margaret, was the only one of my eight office staff already in position so I lost no time in advertising the various jobs and getting people appointed. Apart from Margaret, there was only one other in the batch with previous stores experience, but this turned out to be no bad thing in the end since I could train them without any resistance from past experience.

Morale was good at Inverurie after their recent escape from the death list. One of Beeching's right-hand men, Sir Stuert Mitchell, turned up to assure Bob Garden over a dram in the Kintore Arms that: "There will always be a works at Inverurie as long as there's a railway line north of Aberdeen."

On the whole the men were of a higher calibre than the men at St Rollox and Cowlairs. One incident high-lighting this happened when three wagons of timber turned up in the daily shunt. I told the shunter to take them round to the Timber Shed while I saw about getting them unloaded.

Later that morning I went round to the Timber Shed to find nothing there.

"Where's that three wagons of timber I sent round this morning?" I asked the storeman, Alec Machray.

"Emptied and away," said Alec.

"Who emptied them...?" I asked.

"Me," said Alec, much to my astonishment.

Down in Glasgow it would have taken half a day to negotiate piece-work terms with the shop delegates before we even thought about getting the wagons unloaded.

A couple of years later another two wagons of timber rolled in on the first Monday of the annual holiday fortnight. By this time we were being charged £2 per day for any wagon we did not empty within twenty four hours of receipt. A bureaucratic exercise, of course. No way was anyone getting any money out of my pocket. But I was already building my reputation for effiency — not to say eccentricity — and Inverurie had a 100% record for emptying wagons within twenty four hours. Keeping these wagons for two weeks till my men came back would blow a hole in that.

So I phoned my opposite number at Barassie Works, John Barr — the same man I'd taken over from at Inverurie — proposing that I would label the wagons to him at Barassie. When he got them he would turn them round and label them back to me and by that time my men would be back at work.

"I don't know what you're worrying about," sighed John.

"But anything you say, if it will keep you happy."

But when the wagons arrived at Barassie one of them turned out to be defective, and John's men had to transfer the timber into a fresh wagon. John wasn't too pleased since the wagons should never have been there in the first place and he had to do some creative book-keeping to cover the cost of the transhipment. But I wasn't worried. Inverurie's record was intact and that was all that mattered.

Inverurie Loco Works was small enough to keep a close, overall control on all supplies matters and my performance in the job made the powers-that-be down at Derby sit up and take notice, especially when compared with the records of my blue-eyed contemporaries, some of whom were not doing so well.

The secret lay in having the experience. No matter what crisis arose, I had been there before and knew the way out.

But I still had to be alert for those who would seek to shift the blame for their own shortcomings on to my department. "Shortage of materials" was still the favourite alibi. They tried it on me at Inverurie once when the Trimming Shop was re-upholstering an elderly brake-third coach. There was none of that particular moquette left anywhere on BR and if I couldn't produce a few yards of it the whole coach would have to be done — a terrible waste since only one compartment needed attention. In those days standards were still high and the moquette pattern had to be the same throughout the coach.

I knew from my Operating days that guards' seats in those coaches were usually upholstered with the same moquette as the passengers' seats so I told them to rip this out for the compartment and re-upholster the guards' seats with anything handy. They knew this already down in the Trimming Shop, of course, but needed an alibi for some other shortcoming.

Eastfield Motive Power Depot down in Springburn depended on me a lot for certain types of spares and I had to keep a close eye on them. An 'Engines standing at 6am report' was issued daily by the Chief Mechanical and Electrical Engineer for Scotland and I contrived to get a copy of this. When a loco was stopped for a periodic examination the other fitters were liable to grab any item from it they needed that might be scarce so that by the time the original loco had finished its examination, several parts would be missing. So the loco then appeared on the daily list as 'Waiting material from Inverurie'. I read the riot act at this and complained strongly to Derby headquarters, refusing to accept responsibility since the loco had already been out of traffic for several days.

One day I was at Inverurie Station to meet Fred Howard of the regional supplies department. Fred was an old friend from earlier days and when he got off the train he said:

"You'd better run. There's two men from Eastfield on that train. They say they've got a gun and intend to shoot you."

I took that as a compliment.

The art of one-upmanship entered my sphere of work as it does elsewhere. One day a would-be exponent of this came on the phone from Glasgow.

"James," he said — a bad mistake for a start. I was always 'Jimmy' to everyone except teachers, ministers and income tax inspectors.

"James — catalogue number so-and-so. What is your stock...?"

"Nane o' your flamin' business!" I replied, hanging up my phone.

A few moments later the phone rang again.

"Jimmy," said the same voice, with a pleading note to it this time.

"We're in a bit of a hole. Dae ye think ye kin help us oot...?"

That was different, wasn't it...?

A few years back I called into Scotrail House in Glasgow and the staff there proudly showed me all their modern computers where all you had to do was type in a catalogue number and the entire UK-wide position would come up before your very eyes — who had stock, what was paid for it, who had stock on order, lists of suppliers, lead times. Everything you could possibly want to know.

But I was unimpressed.

"Nae use to me," I said, shaking my head.

"My stock depended a lot on who was asking."

If the enquirer was a friend, then certainly, I would pull out all the stops. But if he'd ever done me a bad turn that might be different.

Very likely I would be out of stock myself and waiting supplies coming in!

A Box For Draff

One thing that took me aback at Inverurie was the practice of selling condemned vehicles — down in Glasgow we just burned them.

My first afternoon there I was startled when two farmers came to my office looking for 'a box for draff.'

A what...?

Fortunately Margaret speedily translated their request to a condemned wagon suitable for holding animal feed, or draff, from the local distilleries. When the cost of repairing a vehicle exceeded a predetermined limit it had the dreaded cat's face — a cross within a circle — painted on it and I had to sell it. Cost was £21.17.6 (£21. 87^1/$_2$) for a covered goods van, £16 for a cattle truck and £1.5.0. (£1.25) per foot for others.

About twelve vehicles a week left Inverurie, going mainly to farmers, and some can still be seen dotted round the countryside acting as livestock shelters or feed stores. Two local contractors took them out and how they managed to deliver them I never did find out. One man and a boy and some old oil drums and sleepers and they could put your van down in any corner you desired. We cut off the buffers and undercart and loaded the old vans with the works crane, but after that it was up to them.

The old vehicles were scattered all over the works and when the farmers turned up I had to show them round, and, of course, they had to see every last one before they would make up their minds. And they always seemed to appear when it was raining.

"Of course they do," said Margaret when I complained.

"Can't do anything on their farms in this weather, can they...?"

Right enough. But this is another thing I set about reorganising.

I appointed a Stores Foreman and gave him the job of selling the vans. Also, I had all condemned vehicles lined up in the siding nearest the street so that the farmers — and their families — would not have to trail all over the works with the attendant danger of being knocked down by rolling stock and engines on the move. Finally, I restricted choice to the first three vehicles in the line.

But the farmers were no mugs. Some of the vans were in better condition than others and, not unnaturally, the farmers wouldn't take one with a broken door or a hole in the roof, preferring to come back another day.

This became a problem since I couldn't afford to pay men to break up the rejected vehicles — or even burn them as we did in Glasgow.

So I put the price up to £30 per van and knocked a few pounds off any that were broken.

They sold like hot cakes!

But somebody down at Derby noticed we were taking in more than the regulation price and came all the way to Inverurie to investigate.

"Listen," I said as soon as he declared his business.

"I'm trying to make some money for British Railways and if you or anyone like you tries to stop me I will phone the Press & Journal in Aberdeen and tell them all about it."

My threat was enough. He went back to Derby and I never heard any more about it.

I wasn't long at Inverurie when Mintlaw chemist Alec Murdoch came to see me.

Apparently the last surviving wagon belonging to the Great North of Scotland Railway was standing in death row awaiting the breakers' torch and Alec wanted to save it. The single-plank wagon had been used as a runner for the Kittybrewster steam crane which explains why it had survived through LNER days and into my time at Inverurie.

I sold Alec the wagon for £6, the cheapest I could make it and still keep my job, but our problems were only beginning. He wanted the wagon down at the Scottish Railway Preservation Society's museum at Falkirk but funds did not run to road transport. I knew the Goods Agent at Falkirk Grahamston was a fellow-enthusiast so I covertly arranged that I would send the wagon to him by rail and he would hand it over on the quiet.

I launched the old wagon into the stream of traffic but it only got the length of Aberdeen before some alert wagon examiner spotted it and returned it to Inverurie 'For Repair'. But how could we repair a wagon already condemned? I twisted some arms in the Wagon Shop and got the wagon at least fit enough to pass old hawk-eye in Aberdeen. She made it to Falkirk at the second attempt and some time later I was pleasantly surprised to learn that I had been made an Honorary Life Member of the SRPS for my part in this humanitarian exercise.

Many years later Margaret and I went down to the 1988 Garden Festival in Glasgow. One of the exhibits was an old saddle-tank pug engine heading a rake of preserved vehicles and I was delighted to see there, standing proudly in line, my wee wagon from 1964.

There was a notice up saying 'Do Not Touch' but nobody was looking and I could not resist ducking under the ropes to give my old pal a clap on her gnarled timbers just for auld lang syne.

A Run With 60012

Inverurie was still repairing steam engines when I arrived — mainly ex-LNER J39s — and there was a scrap Gresley 'Pacific' A4 standing up the yard half dismantled. Unfortunately I did not get its number but it was definitely a streamlined Gresley.

A night shift serviced the fleet of DMUs running on the Buchan lines and the Deeside line and the Erecting Shop were working on the GNSR batch of NB Type 2s. It is a tribute to the skills of the Inverurie men that this lot had a better record in service than the earlier Eastern Region locos. In fact, Alec Munro used to boast that he had all twenty of them running in service for all of twenty four hours — once.

The odd Gresley 'Pacific' from the Aberdeen-Glasgow service sometimes came out for a casual repair, such as 60012, 'Commonwealth of Australia'. She was a devil to slip and I remember one Friday night going home to Glasgow with Peter Lamont on the 5.15pm train when we thought we weren't going to get past Ferryhill. It was a wet night and I felt sorry for the poor fireman as his fire was blown skywards in a succession of thunderous slips.

But we got away eventually and everything seemed to be going well till, just south of Perth, Peter sat up and started sniffing. We both smoked and the air in our first class compartment was pretty thick, so how he could smell anything but tobacco smoke beats me.

"She's running the white metal in her middle cylinder," said Peter in answer to my raised eyebrow.

These locos were prone to run hot on the middle cylinder, and a special lubricant had been developed which gave off a pungent odour to warn drivers before too much damage was done. Sure enough, we stopped at the first lineside phone and Peter was out of the train and up to the footplate to see what was what.

"Right enough," he confirmed when he returned to the compartment. "We'll carry on at reduced speed and get a fresh engine at Stirling."

At Stirling the disabled Gresley limped off to the shed but we both sat up and took notice when we saw who was backing down to take us the rest of the way — NB Type 2 Number 6122. She had been given a shops overhaul in her original condition to compare her with 6123 which had been fitted with a Paxman Ventura engine.

Peter Lamont was greatly excited at this.

"Watch my bag," he said.

"I'll go through to the footplate."

I was a bit miffed at this, since I would have liked a run through on the footplate myself, but I was left on my own for the rest of that particular trip.

I returned on Sunday evenings with the 5.15pm from Glasgow which was worked by a pair of BRCW Sulzer Type 2s (Class 26). These usually worked the Aberdeen-Edinburgh run but we always had them on Sundays.

No on-train buffet but there was a barrow selling tea at Perth and I joined the mad scramble for a cup — until one night I dropped off and awoke as we were entering Forfar. After that I carried my own flask.

Norman Fraser of Arbroath — a former Inverurie Locos man and steam enthusiast — bought 'Morayshire', an ex-LNER 4-4-0 D49, which we painted in her original colours in the shops but the steam engine repairs gradually declined as we shifted on to diesels with the English Electric Type 1s (Class 20), BR-Sulzer Type 2s (Class 25) and the NB Type 2s, all of which had now been transferred from St Rollox for maintenance.

We got one NB Type 2 to re-engine and made such a good job of it that in the end we did more of the re-engining work than St Rollox.

On the Carriage and Wagon side we usually managed to get a sufficient flow of work, although I did feel a bit uneasy when I noticed they were working train loads of carriage repairs to us from the English Midlands.

The last steam engine of all to visit Inverurie Loco Works was 60007, 'Sir Nigel Gresley', sent out from Ferryhill for a casual repair.

The driver must have sensed the importance of the occasion for he blew his whistle all the way back to Aberdeen.

There were always scare stories going about saying the Works were going to close but we didn't pay much attention to them. Hadn't they allocated money to provide new toilets and fence the place? Maybe, but there were straws in the wind that made the more thoughtful among us ponder a bit.

First, they sold off the Paint Shop and forced the painters to squeeze into the Carriage Shop. Next, they cancelled the order for a new switchboard for the works. Then, when manager Bob Garden retired early through ill-health, the man we got in his place, Mr Vincent Spencer, was nearing retirement himself. He came to us from Darlington where he had been Assistant Works Manager for many years under a succession of managers. No disrespect to Mr Spencer, but he was hardly going to set the heather on fire, was he...?

I overcame the shadow on my reputation over the NB Type 2 affair and acquired a name as the best supplies man on the ground. They even offered me promotion to Shildon Works but I was quite happy at Inverurie.

My wife, Margaret, belonged to Inverurie and when our daughter, Marianne, was born in 1967 I decided to withdraw from the rat-race and drop anchor.

The Axe Falls

Come October, 1968, the blow fell. We were to close.

Typically, the bad news came not from official sources but through a phone call to Shop Steward Toby Annand from union headquarters in London. Politicians of every hue hurried to Inverurie to assure us it wasn't their fault. TV and radio crews interviewed us and protest marches were organised through the town. But, as Adam Johnston remarked on Inchbelly Crossing years before, it did no good.

Some men transferred to Barassie Works in Ayrshire only to have to move on again when it closed in 1970. Some found other work in Aberdeen, some retired prematurely, but a great many had to make the long trek down to the Employment Exchange at the foot of the town to sign on and draw the dole for the first time in their lives. House prices tumbled and depression clouds gathered over the proud capital of the Garioch.

But the writing was on the wall from that black day in March ,1963, when Dr Beeching produced his infamous report.

From 124 stations still active on the GNSR, only three were to be left — Inverurie, Insch and Huntly. Protests delayed things for a while but once the closures went through Inverurie's fate was sealed.

Who to blame...?

Well, I'm no politician but if it was a Conservative government that appointed Beeching, it was a Labour administration that carried out his recommendations with Barbara Castle the Minister of Transport who signed the order closing the Great North of Scotland as we knew it.

I can never forget that, even if it means that I can no longer vote for either of the main political parties with a clear conscience.

The best of our men secured other jobs right away so we had to make do with what was left as the main shops began to close down one after another. Much of the material I was loading away was valuable non-ferrous metal, a prime target for the thieves that abounded in the yards between Inverurie and the south. Regulations said I should seal such vans with a metal hoop seal but this was tantamount to telling the crooks which vans to tackle. I thought about not sealing any but that was too big a risk. So I sealed the lot — more than five hundred of them.

Also loading away were the spares for the NB Type 2 that I had taken into St Rollox back in 1960. Like the Ancient Mariner with his albatross, they had followed me to Inverurie, and now I loaded them up for the last time and sent them off down the line with an old railwayman's curse to speed them on their way.

But what was to happen to me and my small family?

Anytime I spoke to Mr MacLean at Derby he assured me I would be 'alright' but as the months went by, several jobs that would have suited me went to others less able and I was forced reluctantly to the conclusion that I did not figure very prominently in whatever lay ahead for British Railways Workshops.

In the end I decided to take matters into my own hands.

The sub-postmaster's job and accompanying shop at Portsoy were advertised for sale and by selling my house and mustering my savings I made the asking price and finally shook the dust of the railways off my heels on Thursday. 19th February, 1970.

Now What...?

With hindsight it is obvious the steam-and-paraffin-oil railway could not have survived into modern times.

Steam engines were shopped every 50,000 miles — two Intermediate Repairs followed by a General Repair. Diesels only went to the works after 150,000 miles at the start, later increased to 500,000 miles, while the latest electric locomotive only requires a workshops-type overhaul every ten years.

Modern technology extended the coaches and other rolling stock's time away from the works, too, so that British Railways Workshops' capacity would have had to be reduced come what may.

But we had the finest railway system in the world until Beeching and his successors got their hands on it.

I blame a combination of pro-road and anti-railway governments, inept and closure-minded management and bloody-minded trade unions.

At the time of the Deeside Railway closure in the mid-sixties a confidential letter from BR management was leaked to me in which the phrase 'if we are successful' was used. But 'successful' at what? Keeping the line open and making it profitable? Not on your life! The context made it clear the aim was closure. I could hardly believe it! No serious attempt was ever made to cut operating costs or work the branch on the 'one-engine-in-steam' (or, if you prefer it, 'one-diesel-in-fume') principle.

About the same time a team from the south descended on Black Bob Gray when he was Operating Assistant at Aberdeen telling him they would be lifting most of his sidings at Aberdeen Joint Station.

"But where will I keep my spare coaches...?" asked a bewildered Bob.

"You won't have any spare coaches!" he was told.

Blinkered union leaders took the work force into a succession of futile strikes over things like 'flexible rostering' that cost the railways much goodwill. For years 'firemen' could be seen in the cabs of the two NB Type 2s allocated to banking trains out of Queen Street station in Glasgow reading newspapers with their feet up on the driving tables.

They had little or no work to do but had to be there because of antiquated agreements dating back to steam days. The sight of these employees lounging in the engine cabs while rail fares rose remorselessly year after year did nothing to enhance the public's opinion of the railways and the men who work in them.

Travelling Ticket Collectors were abolished to reduce the wages bill despite the fact that they brought in several times more than their wages each week in uncollected fares with the result that fare-dodging and out-of-class travel became endemic.

Dr Beeching is now long-gone but the closure mentality he brought to us lives on. A great fuss is made when the odd station is re-opened but the overall picture is one of relentless diminution in the quality of the service offered.

The Aberdeen-Glasgow service now runs every hour but with what...?

Usually a two-coach toy-town train called a 'Sprinter' with cramped, hard seats and little luggage space. A trolley offers tea or coffee in plastic cups at extortionate rates and the two toilets are often flooded or out of order. Contrast that with what we used to have. Ten coaches with twenty or thirty toilets running four times a day offering a full restaurant car service with silver-service morning coffee served at your seat. I know which I would prefer!

So far as I can see Privatisation is just a round-about way of closing all but the Inter-City services from Glasgow and Edinburgh to the south that might be made to show a profit.

We can only wait and see but when ScotRail are so strapped for cash that they cannot afford to paint the Forth Bridge the outlook is anything but rosy.

After The Railways...

Today Springburn is only a ghost of the Railway Capital of the World it once was when it had four building works and two running sheds. Most of the tenements that housed the work-force are gone, as is Cowlairs Co-operative Society that was founded by men from Cowlairs Works who took Wheatley's 4-4-0 Number 224 that went down with the Tay Bridge in 1879 as their emblem. New houses are springing up in the Hydepark grounds but it has to be said that some parts resemble a moon-scape nowadays.

A sad change from the great days when dignitaries from all over the world beat a path to Springburn to order their steam engines.

People like the His Exalted Highness, the Nizam of Hyderabad, an Indian potentate who left such an impression on Springburn that his doings have become part of local folk-lore.

Apparently he wanted a head-on collision organised at high-speed for his delectation but it had to be pointed out, respectfully, that this could not be done, even though he was perfectly prepared to pick up the tab. Next he enquired how we executed murderers in this country.

"We hang 'em" he was told.

"Well, here," said His Exalted Highness, grabbing the nearest member of his entourage.

"Hang him and let me see how it's done."

Again, we had respectfully to decline.

They say he was in the Hydepark managing director's office above the main gate in Vulcan Street one day at 12 noon when the lunch-time

81

whistle blew and all the men hurried up the street for their dinner.

"Look!" cried the Nizam excitedly.

"All your slaves are escaping!"

"Never mind, Your Highness," smiled the MD indulgently.

"They'll be back."

Sure enough, at one o'clock the whistle blew again and the workforce trooped back in.

"Now, Your Highness," said the MD.

"What about this engine you're wanting...?"

"Never mind the engine," cried the Nizam.

"How much do you want for that whistle...?"

Inverurie, on the other hand, has gone onto great things since the Loco Works closed — indeed one local businessman told me he thought the closure was the best thing that ever happened to Inverurie.

I wouldn't go that far myself, but it is a fact that the town soon picked itself up again after the works horn moaned over Inverurie for the last time on the 31st of December, 1969.

North Sea oil helped, of course, but local firms like William Hay and Sons, the soft drinks firm, and Thomas Tait's paper mills continue to prosper. The discarded Loco Works were sold to Aberdeenshire County Council at the give-away price of £25,000 and are now occupied by incoming employers like Messrs Cruickshank and Partners while John Taylor's Versatile Steel Works have moved into larger premises in North Street.

Apart from local industry, Inverurie is becoming very popular as a dormitory town. Inverurie Academy takes its pupils up to university level and the many excellent shops make the town largely self-contained.

On Saturdays and holidays the town positively booms with activity and Inverurie has the air of a town looking forward with confidence to prospects brighter than at any time in its long history.

Dandruff And Malaria

Years ago an old signalman told me:

"Railways is like gettin' dandruff or malaria — once you've got it you never really get rid of it."

And so it has turned out with me.

Any time I spot a train I have to count the vehicles and look for the tail lamp. I just can't help it. And if I'm on Inverurie Station when a train comes in I have to get the doors closed and see it away again as quickly as possible.

As a former naval person I sometimes go about the railways in a black blazer and yachting cap and it's amazing the number of times the public seek my help, thinking I am still an active railwayman. Once at King's Cross a couple of Chinese gentlemen begged me to find their reserved seats for them. I was happy to oblige, of course, even if I didn't get a tip for my trouble. Maybe they thought I was too important to to be offered a reward...?

When it comes to filling in the 'occupation' slot on a passport application form there are many trades I could list — sailor, musician, businessman, exciseman and writer and broadcaster, to name but a few.

But I would have no hesitation in writing 'RAILWAYMAN' — and proud of it!

Many of my railway contemporaries have now booked off for the last time and gone to join the Great Railwayman in the Skies, and I have even completed my own allotted three-score-and-ten shift.

But with luck I may be allowed to go on to do a spot of overtime and as I take my slippered ease by the fireside I sometimes day-dream that one day the phone will ring with an urgent message from British Railways:

"Come back, Jimmy. It's all been a ghastly mistake. We still need you!"

And would I go back...?

You bet I would!

Anytime you like!!